GW01182741

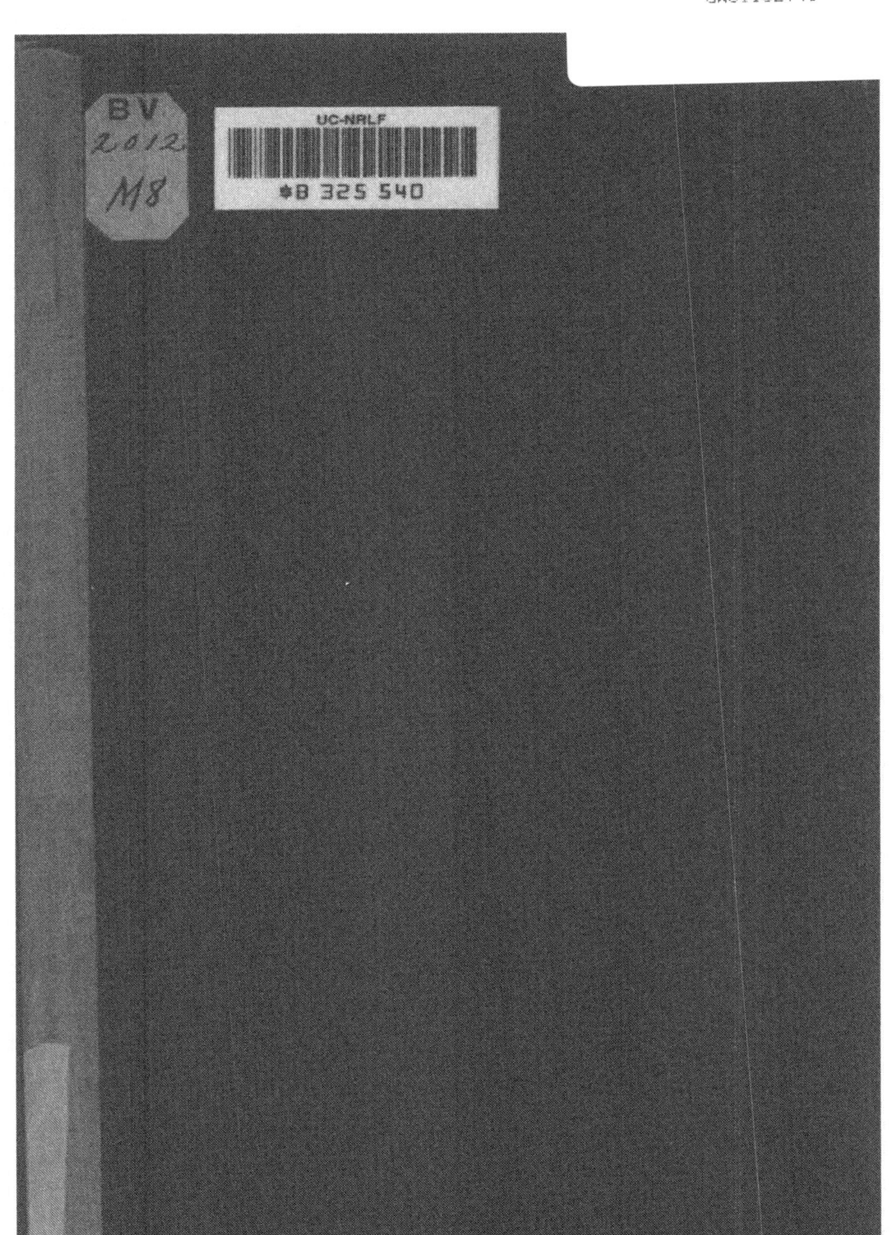
BV
2012
M8
UC-NRLF
$B 325 540

GIFT OF
SIGILLVM · VNIVERSITATIS · CALIFORNIENSIS
FIAT LVX
MDCCCLXVIII
EX LIBRIS

A Selected Bibliography *of* Missionary Literature

The following list aims to present a moderate working library under each section. Consequently a number of titles have been duplicated. A few books are included, especially among those dealing with mission countries, which, though not distinctly missionary, are of special value as describing the setting and conditions of the missionary problem. Pamphlets and magazine articles are of necessity omitted, although some of the most valuable missionary material appears in these forms.

For the convenience of individuals and classes studying home missions a list of books dealing with various North American problems is included, and for prospective foreign missionaries a special list of books on education, prepared by Dr. T. H. P. Sailer. To meet a frequent demand the titles of a few foreign missionary books which should be in a pastor's library are given in a separate group. For an ampler bibliography of foreign missions the student is referred to Volume VI of the Report of the World Missionary Conference.

The Student Volunteer Movement will gladly take counsel with any who desire to add to their missionary libraries from time to time. Any of the books named in this bibliography may be ordered through the Movement. Remittance should accompany order.

GENERAL REFERENCE

BARNES, LEMUEL C. Two Thousand Years of Missions Before Carey. pp. 504. 1900. Christian Culture Press. $1.50.

Deals with the genesis, distribution, and continuity of missions from apostolic times to Carey; a book of reference and study, rather than of easy reading; primary sources used to a large degree, hence the book is authoritative.

BARTON, JAMES L. The Missionary and His Critics. pp. 235. 1906. Revell. $1.00.

Answers the current criticisms of the foreign missionary enterprise, not only by facts and arguments, but by quotations from unprejudiced observers whose words command respectful hearing.

BARTON, JAMES L. The Unfinished Task. pp. 211. 1908. S. V. M 35 cents, 50 cents.

An introductory study of the present problem of evangelizing the world, written by one of the leading missionary experts in North America; states in a masterly way the meaning of the problem, the territory to be occupied, the difficulties to be overcome, and the grounds for confidently expecting success.

BARTON, JAMES L., WHERRY, E. M., and ZWEMER, S. M., editors. The Mohammedan World of To-day. pp. 302. 1907 Revell. $1.50.

Papers read at the First Missionary Conference on Missions to the Mohammedan World, held at Cairo, 1907, invaluable as a summary of the situation before the Turkish revolution.

BASHFORD, J. W. God's Missionary Plan for the World pp. 178 1907. Eaton & Mains 75 cents

A suggestive treatment of the Divine Providence and missions, largely based on the teaching of Scripture.

BEACH, HARLAN P. New Testament Studies in Missions. pp. 40. 1907. (Interleaved.) Association Press. 15 cents.

Outline studies covering the main missionary teachings of the four Gospels, the Acts, and the Pauline Epistles.

BEACH, HARLAN P. A Geography and Atlas of Protestant Missions. Vol. I., pp. 571; Vol. II., pp. 54; 18 double maps. 1901. S. V. M. $4.00.

General account of the environment, forces, distribution, methods, problems, results and prospects of Protestant missions at the beginning of the twentieth century.

BLISS, EDWIN M. The Missionary Enterprise. pp. 406. 1908. Revell. $1.25

A condensed and well-arranged history of missions; a revision and enlargement of the author's previous work, "The Concise History of Missions"; valuable for general information.

BOONE, ILSLEY. The Conquering Christ. pp. 338. 1909. Bible Study Publishing Company. 40 cents.

A comprehensive series of outline studies in missions, of much value to classes or individuals desiring to pursue a nine or twelve-months' course of study; arranged in three parts. Non-Christian Religions and Christianity Compared, Modern Progress of Christianity, and Principles of Missionary Practice and Fruits of Christian Conquest

BRACE, C. L. Gesta Christi. pp. 496 1893. Doran. $1.50.

Review of the influence of Christianity in modifying social conditions in the Roman Empire

Brown, Arthur J. The Foreign Missionary. pp. 412. 1907. S. V. M. 68 cents, $1.50.

Unequalled word pictures of the missionary before sailing and at work on the field; his aims, motives, and qualifications; his problems and his relationships; thoroughly sensible and very informing.

Buckley, James M. Theory and Practice of Foreign Missions. pp. 151. 1911. Eaton & Mains. 75 cents.

Four lectures discussing some of the principles and practical problems of present-day missions; by a noted leader of missionary thought and activity in America.

Call, Qualifications and Preparation of Missionary Candidates, The. pp. 248. 1906. S. V. M. 35 cents, 50 cents.

A collection of papers prepared for periodicals and for Student Volunteer Movement Conventions by different writers, each one of whom is fitted to give helpful advice to those preparing for the foreign mission field and reliable information to all interested in the theme indicated by the title.

Canada's Missionary Congress. pp. 368. 1909. Canadian Council L. M. M. $1.00.

Report of the National Missionary Convention of Canadian laymen at Toronto, in 1909; records an historic event in the missionary enterprise.

Canton, William. A History of the British and Foreign Bible Society. 5 vols. 1910. Murray. Vols. I and II, 15s. each; vols. III, IV, V, 30s. net.

An interesting, full and most valuable review of the first hundred years of the greatest Bible Society, the British and Foreign; glimpses of the work at home and in the many lands where its Bibles are sold.

Carus-Wilson, Mrs. Ashley. The Expansion of Christendom pp. 338. 1910 Hodder & Stoughton. 6s.

An interestingly-written volume, analyzing the motives for foreign missions, sketching the achievements of the enterprise and surveying the present crisis and opportunity which confront it.

Carver, William O. Missions in the Plan of the Ages. pp. 289. 1909 Revell. $1.25.

Sets forth in a scholarly, systematic, progressive way the place of missions in the plan of God as revealed in Scripture.

China Centenary Missionary Conference Records (Report of Shanghai Conference). pp. 823. 1908. American Tract Society. $2.50.

A record of the proceedings at the notable Shanghai Conference of 1907; able papers and keen discussions, by missionaries of distinction, on the great problems before the Christian Church in China; a volume of exceptional value to missionaries to China and to students of Chinese missions.

Church and Missionary Education, The. pp. 320. 1908. Missionary Education Movement. $1.25.

Report of the Convention of the Young People's Missionary Movement held in Pittsburg, 1908.

Clarke, William Newton. A Study of Christian Missions. pp. 268. 1900 Scribner. $1.25.

A thoughtful study of the principles and problems of missions; exhibits originality and careful discrimination

Cook, Charles A. Stewardship and Missions. pp. 170. 1908. American Baptist Publication Society. 35 cents, 50 cents.

A study of the acquisition and disposition of wealth and the possibilities and rewards of true stewardship, both for individuals and churches; specially strong emphasis on the spiritual reactions of generous giving, prepared for use as a text-book.

Dennis, James S. Christian Missions and Social Progress 3 vols. pp. 468; 486; 475. Various dates. Revell. $2.50 a volume.

A monumental work, superior to anything ever published on the social problems confronting missions and the Christian solutions proposed by missionaries, with a most remarkable exhibit of the success attending the work.

Dennis, James S., Beach, Harlan P., and Fahs, Charles H., editors. The World Atlas of Christian Missions. pp. 172. 1911. S. V. M. $4.00

The standard atlas of missions. The maps are well made, and, with the index to mission stations, enable the student of missions conveniently to arrive at his geographical data; the statistics show the missionary work now being carried on in the various mission fields, and are as recent and authoritative as such statistics can well be; includes lists of all Protestant missionary societies.

Dennis, James S. The New Horoscope of Missions. pp. 248. 1908. Revell $1.00.

Four lectures on the new aspects of the missionary question, such as "The New World Consciousness," followed by a thoughtful discussion of "The Message of Christianity to the Non-Christian Religions"; by one of the greatest missionary scholars of the day.

Dwight, Henry Otis, Tupper, H. Allen, and Bliss, Edwin M., editors. The Encyclopedia of Missions. pp. 851. 1904. Funk & Wagnalls. $6.00.

A most useful volume covering almost every phase of missions, being descriptive, historical, biographical, and statistical; best volume of the sort in the English language.

Ecumenical Missionary Conference, New York, 1900. 2 vols. pp. 558; 448 1900. American Tract Society. Out of print.

Addresses delivered at the great Ecumenical Conference of 1900, held in New York; excellent book of missionary reference.

Ellis, William T. Men and Missions. pp. 315 1909. Sunday School Times. $1.00.

A journalist's impressions of the nature, magnitude, and requirements of the missionary enterprise and its special appeal to men, outcome of a visit to mission countries.

Fiske, Martha T. The Word and the World pp. 68. 1907. S. V. M. 25 cents, 40 cents.

Outline studies of typical missionary passages in the Old and New Testaments; arranged for daily study; useful for individual or class work.

Forsyth, P. T. Missions in State and Church. pp. 344 1908. Doran. $1.75.

Ten addresses and sermons by one of the clearest thinkers on missionary questions in Great Britain; very stimulating.

Gairdner, W. H. T. Echoes of Edinburgh, 1910. pp. 281. 1910. Revell. $1.00.

An interpretation rather than a report or summary of the World Missionary Conference; written by a well-known missionary to the Moslems; a convenient document giving the gist and genius of the Conference.

GORDON, A. J. The Holy Spirit in Missions. pp 241. 1893. Revell. 50 cents, $1.25.

Discusses the place of the Spirit in the programme, preparation and fruitage of missionary effort, Bible prophecies concerning missions, and the Spirit's present help.

GOUCHER, JOHN F. Growth of the Missionary Concept. pp. 202. 1911. Eaton & Mains. 75 cents.

Popular lectures on the difficulty, the obligation, the message and the outcome of missions to the non-Christian world.

GULICK, SIDNEY L. The Growth of the Kingdom of God. pp. 221. 1910. Revell. $1.50.

Studies in the growth of Christianity in numbers, understanding, practice, and influence; written by a prominent missionary with a Japanese audience primarily in mind; has apologetic value.

HALL, CHARLES CUTHBERT. The Universal Elements of the Christian Religion. pp. 309. 1905. Revell. $1.25.

The Cole Lectures for 1905 delivered before Vanderbilt University; an attempt to interpret contemporary religious conditions; have apologetic value.

HALL, CHARLES CUTHBERT. Christ and the Human Race. pp. 275. 1906. Houghton, Mifflin. $1.25.

The Noble Lectures for 1906 given by the late President Hall; discuss the attitude of Jesus Christ toward foreign races and religions; reveal a wonderful insight into the beliefs of Orientals.

HALL, CHARLES CUTHBERT. Christ and the Eastern Soul. pp. 208. 1909. University of Chicago Press. $1.25.

The fourth series of Barrows Lectures, delivered in India in 1906-1907; reveal Dr. Hall's intimate and appreciative understanding of the spirit of the Orient and its aptitude for Christianity, especially for the mystical element in Christianity.

HALL, CHARLES CUTHBERT. Christian Belief Interpreted by Christian Experience. pp. 255. 1905. University of Chicago Press. $1.50.

Barrows Lectures reprinted precisely as they were delivered in India; addressed mainly to graduates and undergraduates there and also in Japan; full syllabus; suggestive to young missionaries and to all who emphasize experiential arguments.

HARNACK, A. Mission and Expansion of Christianity in the First Three Centuries. 2 vols. 1906. Williams. 25s.

A full and scholarly account of the development of the missionary movements of the Church in the early centuries of the Christian era, written by a leading German thinker and scholar.

HAYSTACK CENTENNIAL, THE. pp. 364. 1907. A. B. C. F. M. 50 cents.

Report of the gathering at Williamstown, in 1906, called to celebrate the hundredth anniversary of the famous Haystack Prayer Meeting and of historic interest in the impetus which it has given to missionary effort.

HODDER, EDWIN. Conquests of the Cross. 3 vols. pp. 558; 568; 572. 1890. Cassell. Out of print.

A valuable survey of universal missions.

HORTON, ROBERT F. The Bible a Missionary Book. pp. 192. 1905. Pilgrim Press. $1.00.

A study of the missionary teaching of the Scriptures, chiefly of the Old Testament.

HUME, ROBERT A. Missions from the Modern View. pp. 292. 1905. Revell. $1.25.

Views of a famous missionary born in India as to God and the world, the relation of missions to psychology and sociology, what Christianity and Hinduism can gain from each other, and as to how the Gospel should be presented to Hindus.

JACKSON, JOHN. Lepers (Thirty-six Years Among Them). pp 208. Revised 1911. Marshall Bros. 3s. 6d.

An account of the methods and results of thirty-six years' work of the Mission to Lepers in India and the East; covers the work at fourscore stations in India, China, Japan, and Sumatra.

JOHNSON, THOMAS CARY. Introduction to Christian Missions. pp. 220. 1909. Presbyterian Committee of Publication. 75 cents.

Lectures discussing the missionary character and purpose of the Church and sketching, largely through the work of individuals, the progress of the missionary movement from the beginning.

JONES, J. P. The Modern Missionary Challenge. pp. 361. 1910. Revell. $1.50

A distinctive volume on present-day activities and problems of missions; written from the standpoint of the mission field rather than from the academic or administrative standpoint.

KEENLEYSIDE, C. B. God's Fellow-Workers. pp. 312. 1911. Morgan & Scott. 6s.

A deeply spiritual discussion of the missionary enterprise, its basis, motives and requirements; appeals to the loyal and heroic in all Christians for co-operation with the Divine Worker.

KELTIE, J. S., editor The Statesman's Year Book. (An Annual.) pp. 1412. 1911. Macmillan. $3.00.

Contains information which bears on missionary activities from a thousand angles; contents, including statistics, regarded everywhere as authoritative.

LANSDELL, HENRY. The Sacred Tenth. 2 vols. pp. 752. 1906. S. P. C. K. $5.50.

Studies in tithe-giving, ancient and modern, by a British college chaplain; an exhaustive and learned treatment of the subject.

LAWRENCE, EDWARD A. Modern Missions in the East. pp. 340. 1901. Revell. $1.50. (Abridged form. Introduction to the Study of Foreign Missions. pp. 143 S. V. M. 25 cents, 40 cents.)

Though the chapters giving the author's observations on a mission tour of the world are now out of date, his deductions therefrom are a valuable contribution to the science of missions.

LILLEY, J. P. The Victory of the Gospel pp. 371. 1910. Morgan & Scott. 6s.

An excellent treatise on the foreign missionary undertaking, setting forth (a) the Scriptural basis, (b) an apologetic, and (c) the requirements of the enterprise.

LINDSAY, ANNA R. Gloria Christi. pp. 302. 1907. Macmillan. 50 cents.

Covers the wide field of social progress and missions, though necessarily in a cursory way; prepared as a text-book for study classes.

MCLEAN, ARCHIBALD. Where the Book Speaks pp. 241. 1908. Revell. $1.25.

An interesting volume on the Bible as a missionary book, written by a keen student and observer of missions.

MacDonald, J. I. The Redeemer's Reign. pp 299. 1910 Morgan & Scott. 6s.

A modern treatment of the missionary undertaking from the millennarian viewpoint; gives an interesting picture of missionary work in India.

MacLean, Norman. Can the World Be Won for Christ? pp. 194. 1911. Doran. $1.00.

Contains the impressions of some of the great messages of the Edinburgh Conference; exhibits great discernment, reportorial instinct and a right knowledge of missionary problems and methods of the present day.

MacLear, George Frederick. Missions and Apostles of Mediæval Europe. pp. 149. 1897. Macmillan. 25 cents, 40 cents

A study of the mission fields of the middle ages and of the hero apostles who have been the real makers of modern Europe; written by the highest British authority on mediæval missions.

Mabie, Henry C. The Meaning and Message of the Cross. pp. 259. 1906. Revell. $1.25.

A stimulating and suggestive treatment of the truths that lie at the heart of the Christian faith; specially strong statement of the "Missionary Energy of the Cross"; written by one of America's foremost missionary leaders.

Mabie, Henry C. The Divine Right of Missions. pp. 117. 1908. American Baptist Publishing Society. 50 cents.

A brief, logical defense of the right of the Christian Church to propagate its faith among the non-Christian nations; based on the nature of the Christian message and the imperative command of Christ.

Mabie, Henry C. The Task Worth While. pp. 343. 1910. Griffith & Rowland Press. $1.25.

Lectures by a well-known student of the philosophy of missions going to show the place of missions in the plan of God and the urgency of the unfinished task.

Mackenzie, W. Douglas. Christianity and the Progress of Man. pp. 250. 1897. Revell. $2 00.

A strong apologetic for missions, based on the social influence of Christianity; describes the message, methods and results of modern missions.

Men's National Missionary Congress. pp. 800. 1910. L. M. M. $1.00.

The report of the Congress at Chicago, a striking and historical gathering which closed the national campaign of the Laymen's Missionary Movement

Montgomery, H. H., editor. Mankind and the Church. pp. 398. 1907. Longmans. $2 25.

Although strongly Anglican in standpoint, valuable as indicating the contributions to Christian interpretation which may be looked for from the Christian Church of various mission countries, written by seven missionary bishops of the Anglican Church in Britain.

Morgan, G. Campbell. The Missionary Manifesto. pp. 157 1909 Revell. 75 cents.

A series of lectures on the Great Commission; very suggestive.

Mott, John R. The Evangelization of the World in This Generation. pp. 245. 1900. S. V. M. 35 cents, $1 00.

One of the strongest pieces of argumentation in English; has to do with the meaning, obligation, difficulties, possibilities and essentials of world-wide evangelization.

Mott, John R. The Pastor and Modern Missions. pp. 249. 1904. S. V. M. 35 cents, $1.00

Deals with world conditions at the beginning of the twentieth century, and with the pastor as an educational, financial, recruiting and spiritual force in the world's evangelization.

Mott, John R. Strategic Points in the World's Conquest. pp. 218. Revell. 1901. $1 00.

A study in missionary strategics; advocates the adequate missionary occupation of the great educational centers of the non-Christian world that they may become propagating centers for Christianity.

Mott, John R. The Decisive Hour of Christian Missions. pp. 251. 1910. S. V. M. 35 cents, 50 cents, $1.00

The latest work by one of the world's foremost missionary leaders; presents one of the outstanding messages of the World Missionary Conference, namely, the urgency of the present situation in the non-Christian world, and analyzes the necessary conditions whereby the situation may be fully met; a book of unusual power, written as a mission study text-book.

Muir, William. The Call of the New Era. pp. 351. 1910. American Tract Society. $1.25.

An attractively written history of missions both in Bible times and in the succeeding centuries; combines in the study a "scholarly exegesis, broad discrimination and accurate history," and culminates in a stirring presentation of the responsibility and opportunities of the new era of missions.

Murray, Andrew. The Key to the Missionary Problem. pp. 204. 1901. American Tract Society. $1.75.

Discusses the missionary enterprise as a distinctly spiritual one, and by argument and illustration proves that prayer is the great essential for its success.

Murray, J. Lovell. The Apologetic of Modern Missions. pp. 97. Revised 1911. S. V. M. 25 cents.

A study in outline of the common criticisms of missions; objections stated frankly and fairly, and abundant references furnished for answers to the criticisms.

Pfeiffer, Edward. Mission Studies. pp. 279. 1908. Lutheran Book Concern. 75 cents.

Twenty-four scholarly studies in the theory and practice of missions; arranged for text-book use.

Ray, T B., editor. The Highway of Mission Thought. pp 270. 1907. Sunday School Board of Southern Baptist Convention 75 cents.

A collection of eight notable missionary sermons, including William Carey's "Enquiry Into the Obligations of Christians to Use Means for the Conversion of the Heathen."

Richter, Julius. A History of Protestant Missions in the Near East. pp. 435. 1910. Revell. $2.50.

A survey of the history, present condition, and outlook of Protestant missions in Turkey, Persia, and Arabia, written with German thoroughness; deeply interesting; the standard volume on this subject.

Robinson, Charles H. The Interpretation of the Character of Christ to Non-Christian Races. pp. 200. 1910. Longmans. $1.20.

A contribution to the apologetic of Christian missions by the editor of "The East and the West"; contains valuable chapters on the ideals of Hinduism, Buddhism, Confucianism, and Islam.

ROBSON, JOHN. The Resurrection Gospel. pp. 311. 1908. Jennings & Graham. $1.25.

A powerful argument showing the vital connection between the resurrection of Jesus Christ and His command to preach the Gospel everywhere; written by one of the leading missionary authorities in Great Britain.

ROSS, G. A. JOHNSTON. The Universality of Jesus. pp. 124. 1906. Revell. 75 cents.

An examination of the memoirs of Jesus, revealing Him as Representative Man.

SAILER, T. H. P. The Mission Study Class Leader. pp. 140. 1908. Missionary Education Movement. 25 cents.

Pedagogical principles applied to the leading of mission study classes; of decided value for those who wish to become expert in this matter.

SCHMIDT, C. Social Results of Early Christianity. pp. 480. 1900. Pitman 7s. 6d.

A study of the influence of Christianity in bringing about reforms in the political and social life of the Roman Empire; traces in considerable detail the results of the beneficent impact of Christianity on the vices and wrongs of heathen society.

SLATER, T. E. Missions and Sociology. pp. 69. 1908. Elliot Stock. 35 cents.

A valuable monograph on the social bearings and contributions of Christian missions, especially in India; written by a well-known missionary of the London Missionary Society.

SPEER, ROBERT E. Missionary Principles and Practice. pp. 545. 1902. Revell. $1.50.

Discussion by a recognized expert of many fundamental questions of foreign missionary work, lacking in cohesion, but each topic handled with insight and skill.

SPEER, ROBERT E. Missions and Modern History. 2 vols. pp. 358; 356. 1904. Revell. $4.00.

Discusses twelve important movements of the last sixty years affecting missions; closes with "Missions and the World Movement."

SPEER, ROBERT E. Christianity and the Nations. pp. 399. 1910. Revell. $2.00.

A comprehensive treatment of the theory and practice of missions, including such themes as the basis, aims and methods of missions, the problems of the native Church, missions and politics, Christianity and the non-Christian religions, and the unifying influence of missions; written by a foremost missionary authority and leader; Duff Lectures, 1910.

SPILLER, G., editor. Interracial Problems. pp. 485. 1911. King & Son. 7s. 6d.

Contains the papers communicated by acknowledged experts, including missionary experts, to the first Universal Races Congress, held in London, July, 1911; covers a vast range of subjects and has a useful bibliography.

STRONG, WILLIAM E. The Story of the American Board. pp. 523. 1910. Pilgrim Press. $1.75.

An interesting account of the first American missionary society; valuable not only for its historical survey, but because of the graphic sketches which it gives of the men and women who have been connected with it and its revelation of the problems of Board administration.

STUDENTS AND THE MODERN MISSIONARY CRUSADE. pp 713. 1906. S. V M. $1 50.

Report of the Convention of the Student Volunteer Movement held at Nashville in 1906.

STUDENTS AND THE PRESENT MISSIONARY CRISIS pp. 610. 1910. S. V. M. $1.50.

Addresses given at the Convention of the Student Volunteer Movement held at Rochester in 1910.

TAYLOR, ALVA W. The Social Work of Christian Missions. pp. 265. 1911. Foreign Christian Missionary Society. 50 cents.

Indicates with abundant and striking illustrations what Christianity, wherever it goes, does to sanctify the home, exalt woman, care for the child, relieve poverty and physical suffering, develop education and contribute to material progress and the establishing of a substantial and progressive civilization; may be used for class study.

TENNEY, EDWARD PAYSON. Contrasts in Social Progress. pp 421. 1910. Rumford Press. 50 cents.

A study in comparative religions from the standpoint of their social fruits; Hinduism, Buddhism, Confucianism, Mohammedanism, Judaism, and Christianity are considered and the points of contrast include the home, education, literature, moral thought, etc.

THOMPSON, AUGUSTUS C. Moravian Missions. pp. 516. 1882. Scribner. $2.00.

A history to the year 1882 of the aggressive and self-sacrificing missionary work of the Moravian Brethren.

THOMPSON, AUGUSTUS C. Protestant Missions: Their Rise and Early Progress. pp. 314. 1904. S. V. M. 35 cents, 50 cents.

Excellent summary of early Protestant missions; treatment mainly biographical; deals at length with early missions to the two Americas.

WALKER, T. Missionary Ideals. pp. 167. 1911. Church Missionary Society. 1s.

Missionary studies, prepared for class use, in the Acts of the Apostles; written by a prominent missionary of the Church Missionary Society in India, with a view to the practical application of the missionary ideals of the apostolic age to the missionary situation of to-day.

WARNECK, GUSTAV. Outline of a History of Protestant Missions. pp. 435. 1904. Revell. $2.80.

By far the best outline history of missions from the Reformation to the beginning of this century; written by one of Germany's greatest authorities.

WARNECK, JOH. The Living Christ and Dying Heathenism. (Translated from the German.) pp. 312. 1909. Revell. $1.75.

Scientific discussion by a German missionary of ripe experience and scholarship of animistic heathenism and of the forces of the Gospel which are overcoming it, affords a powerful Christian apologetic.

WATSON, CHARLES R. God's Plan for World Redemption. pp. 225. 1911. Board of Foreign Missions of the United Presbyterian Church in North America. 40 cents, 50 cents.

A new contribution to the discussion of the missionary message of the Bible; traces without great detail the progress of the Divine plan in the centuries covered by the Bible narrative; shows in the last two chapters the relation of the individual and the Church to the Divine plan as thus disclosed; written as a textbook for denominational classes of young people by a missionary leader and authority.

WELSH, R. E. The Challenge to Christian Missions. pp. 188. 1902. Allenson. 30 cents, $1.00.

A judicial examination of some of the criticisms of missions; readable and convincing.

WHERRY, E. M, ZWEMER, S. M., and MYLREA, C. G., editors. Islam and Missions pp. 298 1911. Revell. $1.50.

Contains the papers read at the Second Conference on Missions to Moslems, recently held in Lucknow, India, gives an accurate understanding of the present status of this important phase of the missionary undertaking; of interest alike to students of world politics and religions.

WHITLEY, W. T Missionary Achievement. pp. 248. 1908 Revell $1.00.

A concise history of missions sketched on broad lines; assumes a general historical knowledge; discusses some of the present-day problems and opportunities of the missionary enterprise.

WILLIAMSON, J. RUTTER. The Healing of the Nations. pp. 95. 1899. S. V. M. 25 cents, 40 cents.

A simple text-book for mission study classes on the need and the nature of medical missions; contains striking information, especially regarding heathen malpractice.

WORLD MISSIONARY CONFERENCE. 9 vols. 1910 Revell. $5.00; 75 cents a volume.

The most important document on missions in existence, one volume is devoted to each of the Commissions composed of missionary scholars who for eighteen months in advance made painstaking investigations regarding the present-day missionary situation; no such scholarly survey has ever been attempted and no such galaxy of missionary experts has ever collaborated in missionary research as in the case of these Commissions, the reports of the Commissions are entitled as follows:

Volume I.—Carrying the Gospel.
Volume II.—The Church in the Mission Field.
Volume III.—Christian Education.
Volume IV.—The Missionary Message.
Volume V.—Preparation of Missionaries
Volume VI.—The Home Base.
Volume VII.—Missions and Governments.
Volume VIII —Co-operation and Unity.
Volume IX. contains the history and records of the Conference, also a number of addresses.

WORLD-WIDE EVANGELIZATION. pp. 691. 1902. S. V. M. $1.50.

Report of the Convention of the Student Volunteer Movement held at Toronto in 1902.

WORLD'S STUDENT CHRISTIAN FEDERATION CONFERENCE REPORTS

Conference at Williamstown in 1897, Account of. 10 cents.

Conference at Eisenach, 1898, Report of. 50 cents

Conference at Versailles, 1900, Report of. 50 cents.

Conference at Soro, 1902, Report of 50 cents.

Conference at Zeist, 1905, Report of. 25 cents.

Conference in Tokyo, 1907, Report of. 50 cents.

Conference at Oxford, 1909, Report of. 25 cents.

Conference at Constantinople, 1911, Report of. 35 cents.

BIOGRAPHY

BATTERSBY, CHARLES F. HARFORD. Pilkington of Uganda. pp. 316. 1899. Revell. $1 50.

Record of a brief but intense missionary life which worked moral transformations in Uganda; a fitting sequel to the biography of Alexander Mackay.

BLAIKIE, W. GARDEN. The Personal Life of David Livingstone. pp. 508. 1880. Revell. $1.50.

Standard life of Africa's greatest missionary explorer; large use of extracts from Livingstone's writings.

BROWN, GEORGE. George Brown, D.D. pp. 536. 1909. Hodder & Stoughton. $3.50.

Narrative of forty-eight years' residence, travel, and labor of a missionary pioneer and explorer among the Islands of the Pacific; very valuable.

CHAPMAN, J. WILBUR. S. H. Hadley of Water Street. pp. 289. 1906 Revell. $1.25.

Story of twenty years' labors for the spiritual regeneration of the "submerged classes"; wonderful example of success in soul winning amongst the most unlikely.

CLARK, HENRY MARTYN. Robert Clark of the Punjab. pp. 364 1909. Revell. $1.75.

Biography of one of India's pioneer missionaries; contains many characteristic experiences of missionary work among Mohammedans.

CONNOR, RALPH. The Life of James Robertson. pp. 412. 1908. Revell. $1.50

Story of a Scotch Canadian who for twenty-five years was a missionary superintendent in the Canadian Northwest; a rugged, resourceful character, statesman as well as missionary, who laid deep foundations for the Christian development of Western Canada.

DYER, HELEN S. Pandita Ramabai. pp. 197. Revised 1911. Revell. $1.25.

Story of the best-known Indian woman from her childhood to 1900; a record of answered prayers and fulfilled promises in connection with child widow rescue work and famine relief.

ELLINWOOD, MARY G. Frank Field Ellinwood. pp. 246. 1911. Revell. $1.00.

The biography of one of the great missionary leaders and statesmen of the past century, a pioneer student in the field of comparative religion, and for thirty-six years secretary of the Presbyterian Board of Foreign Missions; written in an attractive style by his daughter, with chapters by Miss Ellen C Parsons and Dr. Robert E. Speer.

FAHS, MRS. SOPHIA L. Uganda's White Man of Work pp. 289 1907. Missionary Education Movement 35 cents, 50 cents.

A story, told for young people, of the life and work of a well-known missionary, Alexander Mackay

GAIRDNER, W. H. T. D. M. Thornton. pp. 283. 1909 Revell $1.25.

An inspiring biography, written by a co-worker, of one who in Britain was a leader of the Student Volunteer Missionary Union and in Africa was a tireless worker among educated Moslems, and who incarnated in his life and work the Watchword, "The Evangelization of the World in This Generation"

GRIFFIS, W. E. Verbeck of Japan. pp. 376. 1900. Revell. $1.50.

Life and work of the most influential missionary and publicist that Japan has had, described by one who knew him and his work well.

HAMLIN, CYRUS. My Life and Times. pp. 538 1893. Revell. $1.50.

The life and missionary career of the maker of Robert College, a versatile Yankee whose life story is an inspiration

HAWKER, GEORGE. The Life of George Grenfell pp. 587. 1909. Revell. $2.00.

Biography of one of the most able and devoted and unostentatious of missionaries, who explored and evangelized the Congo country in the spirit and after the method of Livingstone.

HUBBARD, ETHEL DANIELS Under Marching Orders. pp. 222. 1909. Missionary Education Movement. 35 cents, 50 cents.

Story of the life of Mrs. Mary Porter Gamewell, written for young people, relates experiences during the siege of Peking.

JACKSON, JOHN. Mary Reed: Missionary to the Lepers. pp. 127. Revised 1911. Revell. 75 cents.

Impressive sketch of a life spent in the most Christlike of ministries; a satisfactory account of missions among the lepers.

JESSUP, HENRY H. Fifty-three Years in Syria. 2 vols. pp. 404; 428. 1910. Revell. $5.00.

Autobiography of a truly great missionary statesman and pioneer in Syria; acquaints the reader with the forces which are making the new Turkish Empire

JUDSON, EDWARD. The Life of Adoniram Judson. pp. 601. 1904. American Baptist Publication Society. $1.25.

A concise picture, by his son, of the life and work of one of America's most famous missionaries, the apostle to Burma.

LOFTIS, Z. S. A Message from Batang. pp. 160. 1911. Revell. 75 cents.

A simple, intense message from the diary of a young medical missionary of the Foreign Christian Missionary Society; records his long journey to one of the loneliest missionary outposts and gives descriptions of Tibetan life and of the rare opportunities for medical service there; above all reveals the dauntless, devoted spirit of a lion-hearted missionary who laid down his life two months after reaching his field.

LOVETT, RICHARD. James Chalmers: Autobiography and Letters. pp. 510. 1902. Revell. $1.50.

Standard life of one of the most famous and fearless of missionaries to South Sea cannibals, by whose hands he was murdered in 1901.

LOVETT, RICHARD. James Gilmour of Mongolia. pp. 336. Revell $1.75.

An intimate friend's account of the apostle to the Mongols, his unusual character, unique labors, pathetic loneliness, and the lack of perceptible results from his splendid work.

MACCONNACHIE, JOHN. An Artisan Missionary on the Zambesi. pp. 156. 1911. American Tract Society. 50 cents.

Life of a devoted Scottish artisan who labored with the great Coillard on the Zambesi as a pioneer missionary; a manly and saintly personality

MACKINTOSH, C. W. Coillard of the Zambesi. pp. 484. 1907. American Tract Society. $2.50.

The lives of Francois Coillard and Mme. Coillard, of the Paris Missionary Society, devoted pioneer missionaries to Southern Africa, based largely upon letters and memoranda of the Coillards.

MINER, LUELLA. Two Heroes of Cathay. pp. 238. 1903. Revell. $1.00.

The thrilling story, told by the heroes themselves, of their experiences and escape during the Boxer uprising, the first account valuable as an autobiography; the hero of the second has a special interest as a direct descendant of the great Confucius.

NICHOLS, FLORENCE L. Lilavati Singh. pp. 62 1909. Women's Foreign Missionary Society of the Methodist Episcopal Church. 30 cents.

Short life of the noble and brilliant President of the Isabella Thoburn College at Lucknow.

PATON, JAMES. John G. Paton, Missionary to the New Hebrides. pp. 481. 1906. Revell. $1 50

Life of one of the most simple, saintly, and brave of modern missionaries.

PEILL, J. The Beloved Physician of Tsang Chou. pp. 293. 1908. Headley Bros. $2.00.

Memorial, written by his father, of a life laid down at an early age for China; typical of medical missionary work, gives sidelights on the Boxer uprising.

PORTER, HENRY D. William Scott Ament. pp. 377. 1911. Revell. $1.50.

An account, embodying much interesting correspondence, of the life of Dr. Ament of the American Board, for thirty-six years a missionary in China; shows the growth of missionary work in North China and portrays life in the troublous days of the Boxer uprising.

RICHARDS, THOMAS C. Samuel J. Mills. pp. 275. 1906. Pilgrim Press. $1.50.

Interesting biography of the leader of the famous Haystack band at Williamstown; valuable also as an account of the origin of American foreign missionary endeavor.

SINKER, ROBERT. Memorials of Ion Keith-Falconer. pp. 258. 1903. Deighton, Bell & Co. $1.85

Standard account of the short life of one of the most talented and versatile of missionaries, a pioneer in Arabia.

SMITH, GEORGE. The Life of Wm. Carey, D.D. pp. 389 1887. John Murray. 75 cents

SMITH, GEORGE. The Life of Alexander Duff. pp. 383. 1900. Hodder & Stoughton. Out of print.

These two lives—one of the English pioneer, the other of Scotland's most famous educational missionary—are classics. Dr. Duff's life is condensed from an earlier two-volume edition.

SMITH, GEORGE. Henry Martyn: Saint and Scholar. pp 580 1902. Revell. $1.50

Standard life of the most spiritual of early missionaries to India, one whose life has inspired multitudes, despite its occasional morbidness; gives interesting facts concerning early work in Persia also

SPEER, ROBERT E A Memorial of Alice Jackson. pp. 128 1909. Revell. 75 cents

Sketch of the brief life of a Smith College girl, a detained volunteer for foreign missionary work, written by one who knew her intimately

SPEER, ROBERT E. Memorial of Horace Tracy Pitkin. pp. 310. 1903. Revell. $1.00.

Story of a prominent Student Volunteer's work at home, with an account of his brief life in China and his martyrdom in 1900.

SPEER, ROBERT E. The Foreign Doctor. pp. 384. 1911. Revell. $1.50.

Life of Dr. J. P. Cochran, one of the most devoted and able of missionaries to the near East; shows him in the exercise of his unusual medical gifts, in the extension of medical missionary work and in the use of his political influence during the thrilling days of the Kurdish invasion of Persia; a worthy biography of a truly great missionary.

TAYLOR, CHARLES E. The Story of Yates, the Missionary. pp 304. 1900. Sunday-School Board of Southern Baptist Convention. $1.00.

President Taylor tells through letters and by reminiscences the life-story of one of the strongest American missionaries to China; records his contribution to Chinese Christian literature and his great stimulus to missionary work in the South.

TAYLOR, MRS. HOWARD. Pastor Hsi: Confucian Scholar and Christian. pp. 494. 1907. China Inland Mission. $1.50

Perhaps the most remarkable of Chinese Protestant Christians is here pictured vividly; story of his life both before and after conversion.

TAYLOR, DR. AND MRS. HOWARD. Hudson Taylor in Early Years: The Growth of the Soul pp. 532. 1912. Doran. $2.25.

An engrossing recital of the heroism and labors of the founder of the China Inland Mission; the subject and the biographers are equally fortunate in each other.

THOMPSON, RALPH WARDLAW. Griffith John. pp. 544. 1906. Doran. $2.00.

A life-story of one of the most remarkable missionaries to China; record of fifty years of heroic toil and unusual achievement.

TOWNSEND, WILLIAM J. Robert Morrison, Pioneer of Chinese Missions. pp 160. 1902. Revell. 75 cents

Useful sketch of a great pioneer, the centennial of whose arrival was celebrated in China in 1907.

TUTTLE, DANIEL SYLVESTER. Reminiscences of a Missionary Bishop. pp. 498. 1906. Whittaker. $2.00.

Romantic story of a self-sacrificing missionary in Montana, Idaho, and Utah, contains a graphic picture of the Mormon system.

UCHIMURA, KANZO. How I Became a Christian. pp. 199. 1906. Keiseisha. 25 cents.

A striking biography of a Japanese Christian; describes the intellectual as well as spiritual influences which led to his accepting the Christian faith, and the effect of this decision upon his life work; of interest both from a psychological and a religious standpoint.

WELLS, JAMES. Stewart of Lovedale. pp. 419. 1909. Revell. $1.50.

Biography of a prince among missionaries; recounts the varied and untiring efforts of the "long strider," and shows his influence upon the development of South and Central Africa.

WRIGHT, HENRY BURT. A Life With a Purpose. pp. 317. 1908. Revell. $1.50.

Story of the brief but devoted and fruitful career of Lawrence Thurston, both as a student at Yale and as a worker in the Yale Mission in China; written by an intimate friend.

YONGE, CHARLOTTE M. Life and Letters of John Coleridge Patteson. 2 vols. pp. 370; 411. 1894. Macmillan. $3.00.

Standard life of one of Britain's finest spirits, who illustrates better than almost any other the humanity, versatility, attractiveness, scholarship, and spirituality of the missionary calling.

ZWEMER, SAMUEL M Raymund Lull. pp. 156. 1907. Funk & Wagnalls 75 cents

One of three recent biographies of this first missionary to the Moslems, and the best from a missionary standpoint; has a full bibliography and interesting illustrations.

COLLECTED BIOGRAPHIES

BEACH, HARLAN P. Knights of the Labarum. pp 111. 1896. S V. M. 25 cents

Life sketches of Adoniram Judson, Alexander Duff, Dr John Kenneth Mackenzie, and Alexander Mackay; valuable as a text-book.

BEACH, HARLAN P. Princely Men in the Heavenly Kingdom. pp. 244. 1903. Missionary Education Movement. 35 cents, 50 cents.

Brief studies of the following missionaries to China; Robert Morrison, John Kenneth Mackenzie, James Gilmour, John Livingstone Nevius, George Leslie Mackay; a closing chapter on Chinese martyrs of 1900; prepared as a text-book.

CREEGAN, CHARLES and JOSEPHINE GOODNOW. Great Missionaries of the Church. pp 404. 1895. Crowell. $1 50.

The life stories, in a chapter each, of twenty-three of the best-known modern missionaries.

DAWSON, E. C. Heroines of Missionary Adventure. pp. 340. 1908. Lippincott. $1.50.

Short sketches of the lives of Mrs. Alexander Duff, Mrs. Robert Clark, Irene Petrie, Fanny Butler, Mary Reed, Mrs. Hudson Taylor, Fidelia Fiske, Madame Coillard, and other women missionaries less well known.

FIELD, CLAUD. Heroes of Missionary Enterprise. pp. 335. 1907. Lippincott. $1.50.

Life sketches of twenty-eight notable missionary heroes, such as Eliot, Brainerd, Livingstone, Hans Egede, and John Williams; stories illustrating the romance and heroism of missions.

GRACEY, MRS. J. T. Eminent Missionary Women. pp. 215. 1898. Eaton & Mains. 85 cents.

Twenty-eight brief biographies of women-workers in various foreign fields make this the fullest collection of the kind

HOLCOMB, HELEN H. Men of Might in Indian Missions. pp. 352. 1901. Revell. $1.25.

Lives of thirteen famous missionaries of various nationalities, ranging from the first Protestant missionary to Dr. Kellogg, who died in 1899; selection is good, emphasis satisfactory, and treatment fairly full

LAMBERT, JOHN C. Missionary Heroes in Africa. pp. 156 1909. Lippincott. 75 cents

Brief stories illustrating the work of Alexander Mackay, Bishop Hannington, Fred S. Arnot, A. B. Lloyd, Francois Coillard.

LAMBERT, JOHN C. Missionary Heroes in Asia. pp. 158. 1908. Lippincott. 75 cents.

Interesting sketches illustrating the life and work of James Gilmour, Jacob Chamberlain, Joseph Hardy Neesima, George Leslie Mackay, Annie R. Taylor, and Dr. Westwater

McDOWELL, WM. F., and others. Effective Workers in Needy Fields. pp. 195. 1905. S V M. 35 cents, 50 cents.

Short biographies of five missionaries chosen to represent different mission fields and different phases of missionary work—Livingstone, Mackay of Formosa, Isabella Thoburn, Cyrus Hamlin, and Joseph Hardy Neesima; prepared as a text-book.

SHELTON, DON O. Heroes of the Cross in America. pp. 304. 1904. Missionary Education Movement. 35 cents, 50 cents.

Home missionary work set forth attractively through biographies, an added chapter, general in character, widely used as a mission study text-book.

SPEER, ROBERT E Servants of the King. pp. 216. 1909. Missionary Education Movement. 35 cents, 50 cents.

Written for young people; outlines of the lives of eleven well-selected heroes and heroines of the faith, most of them foreign missionaries; adapted to use as a text-book.

SPEER, ROBERT E. Some Great Leaders in the World Movement. pp. 295. 1911. Revell. $1.25.

Inspiring sketches of the lives of six illustrious heroes of the Cross, Raymund Lull, William Carey, Alexander Duff, George Bowen, John Lawrence, and Chinese Gordon, typical of various phases under which the missionary enterprise has been promoted, written by a skillful missionary biographer.

THOMPSON, A. C., and others Modern Apostles of Missionary Byways. pp. 108. 1899. S V M. 40 cents.

In this book Greenland, Fuegia, Hawaii, Mongolia, Ceylon, and Arabia are the picturesque background against which stand out in clear relief the lives of Hans Egede, Allen Gardiner, Titus Coan, James Gilmour, Eliza Agnew, and Ion Keith-Falconer.

WALSH, W. PAKENHAM. Heroes of the Mission Field. pp. 249. Whittaker. $1.00.

Sketches of thirteen missionaries chronologically arranged from the Apostolic times to the close of the eighteenth century.

WALSH, W. PAKENHAM Modern Heroes of the Mission Field. pp. 344. Whittaker. $1.00.

A continuation of the preceding volume; lives of a dozen great missionaries of the nineteenth century, some of them little known

WOLF, L. B. Missionary Heroes of the Lutheran Church. pp. 247. 1911. Lutheran Publishing Society. 75 cents.

A popular sketch of the history of early Lutheran mission work, centering it in the personalities of Ziegenbalg and other great missionaries.

MEDICAL MISSIONS

BARNES, IRENE H. Between Life and Death. pp. 307. 1901. Church of England Zenana Missionary Society 3s. 6d.

Account of the need, methods, incidents and opportunities of woman's medical work, especially in India and China.

BRYSON, MARY ISABEL. John Kenneth MacKenzie. pp. 404. Revell. $1.50.

Standard life of one who is generally regarded as the most illustrious medical missionary to China.

DE GRUCHÉ, KINGSTON. Dr Apricot of Heaven Below. pp. 143. 1911. Revell. $1.00.

An account of the work of Dr. D. Duncan Main, of the Hangchow Medical Mission (C. M. S.); gives a rare insight into the conditions and opportunities of medical missions in China; very interestingly written.

EDWARDS, MARTIN R. The Work of the Medical Missionary. pp. 65. 1909. S. V. M. 20 cents

An excellent outline course for study; broad in scope, and discusses the whole question practically; contains a study of the Master Medical Missionary; useful for individual and class work, bibliography.

HOPKINS, S. ARMSTRONG. Within the Purdah pp. 248. 1898. Eaton & Mains. $1.25.

Bright and faithful descriptions of the Hindu home, and especially of the conditions surrounding zenana women, with an account of the missionary efforts being put forth for the uplifting and redeeming of the women and girls of India.

OSGOOD, ELLIOT I. Breaking Down Chinese Walls. pp. 217. 1908. Revell. $1.00.

Reveals the power of medical missions to remove prejudice and effect an entrance for the Gospel into Chinese homes and hearts.

PEILL, J. The Beloved Physician of Tsang Chou. pp. 293. 1908. Headley Bros. $2.00.

Typical of medical mission work in China; sketches the brief career of an attractive young English doctor; incidental discussion of some of the practical problems of medical missionary work

PENNELL, T. L Among the Wild Tribes of the Afghan Frontier. pp 324. 1909. Lippincott $3 50.

Attractive story of pioneer medical work on the borders of Afghanistan; contains an account of the customs and traditions of the people.

PENROSE, VALERIA F. Opportunities in the Path of the Great Physician. pp. 277 1902. Presbyterian Board. $1.00.

An outline of the medical mission work being done in various countries, with descriptions and illustrations to show the opportunties which await the Christian physician in mission lands

SPEER, ROBERT E The Foreign Doctor. pp. 384. 1911 Revell. $1.50.

Perhaps foremost among the biographies of medical missionaries; gives a graphic idea of the sort and amount of work the medical missionary has to do and of the vast influence he may acquire; shows Dr J. P. Cochran as physician, diplomatist, counsellor and missionary leader in Western Persia, as the "Hakim Sahib" intrenched in the love of the people to whom he gave his life

STEVENS, GEORGE B. The Life of Peter Parker, M. D. pp. 356. 1896. Congregational Sunday School and Publication Society Out of print.

Life story, consisting largely of extracts from letters and journals, of the "father of medical missions," a noted missionary to China.

WANLESS, W. J The Medical Mission pp. 96. 1898 S. V M. 10 cents.

Valuable summary of many phases of the subject, written by a medical missionary; illustrations mainly from India.

WILLIAMSON, J RUTTER. The Healing of the Nations. pp. 98. 1899. S. V. M 25 cents, 40 cents.

Written as a text-book for study classes; shows opportunities for profitable life-service in this calling

WISHARD, JOHN G. Twenty Years in Persia pp. 349. 1908. Revell. $1.50

An interesting record of what a medical missionary alone could observe and experience; one of the best books on Persia.

RELIGIONS

BARTON, JAMES L., WHERRY, E. M., and ZWEMER, S. M. editors. The Mohammedan World of To-day. pp 302. 1907. Revell. $1.50.

Papers read at the First Missionary Conference on Behalf of the Mohammedan World, Cairo, 1906; possesses sociological and political, as well as intense missionary, interest.

BETTANY, G. T. The World's Religions. pp. 908 1891. The Christian Literature Society. $5.00.

A popular review of the religions of the world, including some of the ancient faiths; seven books in one volume.

BROOMHALL, MARSHALL. Islam in China. pp. 332. 1910. China Inland Mission 7s 6d.

A comprehensive and readable account of a Moslem population larger than that of Egypt, Persia or Arabia; treats the modern aspects of this great and little-known question; largely the outcome of investigations made for Commission I of the Edinburgh Conference. Part One is historical, and Part Two deals with present-day conditions; contains valuable appendices on Chinese and Mohammedan literature; unusually full indices and a bibliography of the subject.

DAVIDS, T. W. RHYS. Buddhism pp. 262. 1894. Gorham. 75 cents.

Interesting summary of Buddhism by the foremost British authority; full enough for all but specialists.

DEGROOT, J. J. M. The Religion of the Chinese pp. 230. 1910. Macmillan. $1.25.

Lucid treatment, by a foremost authority, of Taoism, Confucianism, and Buddhism, showing their relationships and their points of fusion; proves that all Chinese religious beliefs have a common animistic basis.

FARQUHAR, J N. A Primer of Hinduism. pp. 187. 1911. Christian Literature Society for India 4 annas.

Foremost treatment of Hinduism in brief compass; outlines its history and gives an analysis of the Hinduism of to-day, reveals unusual scholarship and sympathetic insight; points the way to extended investigations, gives for each subject illustrative readings from the Hindu Scriptures; excellent bibliography and many illustrations; written by a recognized authority.

GAIRDNER, W. H. T. The Reproach of Islam pp 367. 1909. Student Christian Movement 2s 4d.

Text-book on the Moslem world, its present opportunities and its challenge to the Christian Church; prepared by one of the leading missionaries in the intellectual capital of Islam, Cairo

GRANT, G. M. The Religions of the World in Relation to Christianity. pp. 137. Revell. 50 cents.

An interesting discussion of Mohammedanism, Confucianism, Hinduism, and Buddhism, rather generous view of ethnic religions, but not more favorable than men of the liberal school would justify.

GRIFFIS, WILLIAM E. The Religions of Japan. pp. 449 1895. Scribner $2 00

The best work treating of the main religions of Japan in a single volume; written by a specialist on Japan and its religions.

HALL, CHARLES CUTHBERT. The Universal Elements of the Christian Religion. pp. 309. 1905. Revell. $1.25.

An attempt to interpret contemporary religious conditions, makes it clear that Christianity alone has a message for all men

HALL, CHARLES CUTHBERT. Christ and the Eastern Soul. pp. 298. 1909. Univ. of Chicago Press. $1.25.

The Barrows Lectures, delivered in 1906-1907 by Dr. Charles Cuthbert Hall in India, the lectures are irenic, yet loyal to the supremacy and dignity of Christianity, recognize fully all that is good in ethnic religion, and are highly appreciative of the gifts and capacities of the Eastern soul, especially its ability to profit by and exemplify the benefits of the Christian religion, when loyally and intelligently accepted

HOPKINS, EDWARD W. The Religions of India. pp. 612. 1895. Ginn & Co. $2.00.

Professor Hopkins writes as a specialist who has studied in India the various religions prevailing there, in many respects the best comprehensive work on the subject.

HUME, R. A. An Interpretation of India's Religious History. pp 224. Revell. $1.25.

A readable sketch showing the groping of the Hindu mind after God, through the successive steps of progress, arrest, degeneracy, and reform, magnifies the truth to be found in Hinduism and the contribution which Indian thought is to make to the interpretation of Christ and His message; compares the religious development of India and that of the West; written by one of the most experienced and best-known missionaries to India.

JEVONS, FRANK B. Introduction to the Study of Comparative Religion. pp. 283. 1908. Macmillan. $1.50.

A book of great knowledge and penetration; a most satisfactory introduction to the study of comparative religion; lectures given by the Principal of Hatfield Hall, University of Durham, on the Hartford-Lamson Foundation at Hartford Theological Seminary.

KELLOGG, S. H. A. Handbook of Comparative Religion. pp. 185. 1905. S. V. M. 30 cents, 75 cents.

A study in comparative religion by topics, the doctrines concerning God, man, sin, etc., considered according to the teaching of each of the great religions of the world.

KELLOGG, S. H. The Light of Asia and the Light of the World. pp. 390. 1885. Macmillan. $2.00.

A comparative study of Buddhism and Christianity by one who was an authority on both, and who had labored for years in Buddhism's natal land

KNOX, GEORGE W. The Development of Religion in Japan. pp. 204. 1907. Putnam $1 50

Presents with insight and scholarship a brief account of the religions that have invaded Japan, and their influence upon the evolution of the nation; indicates the influence of Christianity in the progress of the New Japan.

LEGGE, JAMES. The Religions of China. pp. 308. 1881. Scribner. Out of print.

Four lectures, by the foremost English ...hority, on Confucianism and Taoism, and on the comparison of both with Christianity

LLOYD, ARTHUR S. Christianity and the Religions. pp. 127. 1909. Dutton. 75 cents.

Three lectures on the essential message of the Christian religion which differentiates it from the non-Christian faiths.

LOVE, JAMES FRANKLIN. The Unique Message and the Universal Mission of Christianity. pp 256 1910. Revell. $1.25.

A contribution to the study of comparative religion emphasizing the points of contrast rather than those of comparison between Christianity and the other religions; of the strongly evangelical school

MACDONALD, D. B. Aspects of Islam. pp. 375. 1911. Macmillan. $1.50.

A splendid introduction to the study of Mohammedanism by one of the greatest scholars and thinkers of the day on that subject; deals with the question practically, showing the essential Islam as the missionary finds it, interpreting the religion and indicating the attitude which the missionary should take towards it and its adherents, the Hartford-Lamson Lectures for 1911.

MACDONELL, ARTHUR A. A History of Sanskrit Literature. pp. 472. 1900. Appleton. $1 50.

A necessarily brief treatment of Sanskrit literature as a whole, a trustworthy statement of the results of Sanskrit research down to the time of publication; not too technical for the general reader; excellent bibliographical notes.

MARGOLIOUTH, D. S Mohammed and the Rise of Islam. pp. 481. 1905. Putnam. $1.50.

Presents an appreciation of the founder of Islam, whose main aim was the solution of an exceedingly difficult political problem; pictures Mohammed as a hero rather than as a prophet; written by an Oxford professor of Arabic, after prolonged study.

MENZIES, ALLAN History of Religion. pp. 438. 1895. Scribner $1 50.

A compendious view of ancient and present-day religions from the modern standpoint; intended for text-book use in colleges, etc.

Methods of Mission Work Among Moslems. Papers read at the Cairo Conference. pp. 236 1906. Revell. $1.00.

A wide range of topics, covering all kinds of missionary work among Moslems; presented by various authorities.

MITCHELL, J. MURRAY. The Great Religions of India. pp. 287. 1905. Revell. $1.50.

The Duff Lectures, given by a veteran who, in India and at home, was a student and authority on Hinduism, Zoroastrianism and Buddhism.

MONTGOMERY, H. H., editor. Mankind and the Church. pp. 398. 1907. Longmans. $2.25.

A symposium by seven missionary bishops of the Anglican Church on the contributions which Christianity may expect from non-Christian peoples when Christianized, and on the attitude in which the non-Christian faiths should be approached.

MUIR, WM., AND OTHERS. Present-Day Tracts on the Non-Christian Religions of the World. pp. 349 1887. The Religious Tract Society. $1.00.

A collection of scholarly presentations of the chief religions of the world in contrast with Christianity.

MYLNE, LOUIS GEORGE. Missions to Hindus. pp. 189. 1908. Longmans. $1.20

A treatment, written with expert knowledge, of caste in India as the social system of the Hindu religion and of the methods whereby the problems of caste should be met; together with an examination of the results of missionary effort in India, written by the Bishop of Bombay.

NAUROJI, DHANJIBHAI. From Zoroaster to Christ. pp. 93 1909. Oliphant. 2s

Story of the conversion and subsequent missionary work of a distinguished Parsee convert in Bombay.

RICHARDS, E. H., and others Religions of Mission Fields as Viewed by Protestant Missionaries. pp. 300. 1905 S. V. M. 35 cents, 50 cents.

Discussion from the viewpoint of the mission field of nine of the most important religions, written by men most of whom have had more than twenty years' experience with those who hold these faiths, valuable as a text-book for mission study classes

RODWELL, J. M Translation of the Koran. pp. 506 Dutton. Everyman's Library. 50 cents, $1.00.

Much better than the translation of Sale and less expensive than that of Palmer; has the advantage of a chronological arrangement of the Surahs.

ROSS, JOHN. The Original Religion of China. pp. 327. 1909 Oliphant. 5s.

A scholarly discussion of the primitive monotheistic and animistic beliefs of the Chinese people, the substratum of the present-day religions of China; written by a Scotch missionary in Manchuria.

Sacred Books of the East Described and Examined. 3 vols. pp. 1357. Various dates. Christian Literature Society for India. Rupees, 1¼.

Summaries of translations of most important Hindu sacred books, with introductions, etc., most valuable for missionaries to India and to others wishing the gist of Hindu teachings. Vol. I contains the Rig-Veda, Atharva-Veda, the Brahmanas of the Vedas; Vol. II contains selections from the Upanishads, the Bhagavad Gita, Vedanta Sara, Yoga Sastra, Laws of Manu; Vol III has the Ramayana, Mahabharata, Vishnu Purana.

SELL, EDWARD B. The Faith of Islam. pp. 366. Second edition. 1896. Kegan, Paul. 12s. 6d.

SELL, EDWARD B. Islam: Its Rise and Progress. pp. 96. 1906 Simpkin, Marshall. 9s

Two books which are invaluable to every student of the subject, the former giving an historical account of the system and the latter dealing with the various articles of faith and some of the present-day sects and movements, written by one who for more than a decade has been a leading authority on Islam.

SHEDD, WILLIAM A Islam and the Oriental Churches. pp. 251. 1904. Presbyterian Board of Publication. $1.25.

Treats of the influence of the Oriental Christian Churches upon the beginnings of Islam and its theology, Islam's government relation to these churches, the expansion of the faiths, the downfall of Oriental Christianity in the common ruin, and lessons for the future, valuable for missionaries to the Levant.

SIMON, GOTTFRIED. Islam und Christentum: Im Kampf um die Erokerung der Animistischen Heidenwelt. pp. 475 1910. M. Warneck. 6 marks.

A very scholarly and timely treatise on the struggle between Islam and Christianity for the conquest of animistic heathendom. Discusses the co-operative factors and religious motives that lead pagans to become Moslems, the social and religious conditions after they become Mohammedan and the conversion of these Moslems to Christianity.

SLATER, T. E. The Higher Hinduism in Relation to Christianity. pp. 291. 1903. Elliot Stock. 85 cents.

A generous interpretation of philosophic Hinduism; written by a scholarly and experienced missionary to the educated classes of India.

SPEER, ROBERT E. The Light of the World. pp. 372 1911. Macmillan. 35 cents, 50 cents.

A study of Hinduism, Buddhism, Mohammedanism, Confucianism, Taoism, Animism, in comparison with Christianity; quotes largely from recognized authorities, contains a chapter giving testimonies from thoughtful Oriental Christians; suitable for advanced mission study classes.

TIELE, C. P. Elements of the Science of Religion. pp. 302. Two series. Scribner $2.00 each.

Standard Introduction to the Science of Religion; Gifford Lectures, delivered in 1896 and 1898 by the Professor of History and Philosophy of Religion in the University of Leyden

SOOTHILL, WILLIAM E. The Analects of Confucius. 1911. Oliphant. 15s.

A new translation of these classics; of much value to those desiring to make a careful study of the religions of China.

TISDALL, W ST. CLAIR. The Noble Eightfold Path. pp. 215. 1903. Elliot Stock. 6s.

In these lectures the religion of Buddha is judged from the standpoint of an evangelical critic, and its philosophy is severely reviewed, perhaps too little credit is given to some of its better features

TISDALL, W. ST. CLAIR. Muhammadan Objections to Christianity. pp. 239. 1904. Gorham. $1.25.

One of the most interesting books for those who desire to know why it is difficult to reach Moslems with the Gospel; a vade mecum for the missionary.

TISDALL, W. ST. CLAIR Comparative Religion. pp. 132. 1909. Longmans. 40 cents.

A Christian apologetic based on a study of certain Christian doctrines and those doctrines of the ethnic faiths which bear a faint or partial resemblance to them.

WARNECK, JOH. The Living Christ and Dying Heathenism. pp. 312 1909. Revell $1 75.

A scientific analysis of animism and a study of the supernatural forces of the Gospel which are conquering it; exceptionally useful

WHERRY, E. M. Islam and Christianity in India and the Far East. pp. 237. 1907. Revell $1.25.

An authoritative account of the spread and character of Islam in India, China and Malaysia, together with the present efforts and results of Christian missions to Moslems in that part of the world.

WHERRY, E. M., ZWEMER, S. M., and MYLREA, C. G, editors Islam and Missions. pp. 298. 1911. Revell, $1 50.

Papers read at the recent Lucknow Conference on Missions to Moslems; every contributor an expert; introductory survey by Dr. Zwemer of exceptional value; indispensable to an accurate knowledge of the present condition of this missionary problem.

WILKINS, W. J. Hindu Mythology. pp. 499. 1882 Thacker. 10s. 6d.

A valuable account of mythological legends pertaining to the Vedic, Puranic, and inferior deities of India.

WILKINS, W. J. Modern Hinduism. pp. 423. 1900. Thacker. 7s. 6d.

An excellent survey of Hinduism, its worship, ethics, social institutions, results and eschatology.

WILLIAMS, M. MONIER. Hinduism. pp. 238. 1894. Gorham. $1.00.

An exceedingly valuable account of the rise and present status of Hinduism, by one of the foremost authorities; many quotations from sacred books; a condensation of the larger and more readable work, "Buddhism and Hinduism"

ZWEMER, SAMUEL M. The Moslem Doctrine of God. pp. 120 1905. American Tract Society 45 cents

Enlightening monograph on a vital doctrine of Mohammedanism, written by a high missionary authority on Islam.

ZWEMER, SAMUEL M. Islam: A Challenge to Faith. pp. 295. 1907. S. V. M. 35 cents, $1.00

A thoroughly reliable account of the rise, spread and present condition of Mohammedanism; an exposition of its practice, ritual and ethics, by one whose scholarship and extended missionary experience give his judgments great weight.

COUNTRIES

AFRICA

BENTLEY, W. HOLMAN. Pioneering on the Congo. 2 vols. pp. 478; 488. 1900. Revell. $5 00.

The best missionary account of the history and life of the Congo tribes; written by a high authority, missionary work and travels also prominent.

BERRY, W. G. Bishop Hannington. pp. 208. 1908 Revell. $1.00.

Life story of an English school boy, "Mad Jim," who became the martyr bishop to Uganda; gives a vivid picture of a pioneer missionary; brightened with many touches of humor and filled with human interest.

BLAIKIE, W. G. The Personal Life of David Livingstone. pp. 508. 1880. Revell. $1 50.

Standard life of Africa's greatest missionary explorer; large use of extracts from Livingstone's writings; one of the greatest of missionary biographies.

CROMER, THE EARL OF. Modern Egypt. 2 vols. pp. 594; 600. 1908. Macmillan. $6.00.

The standard work on the present condition of Egypt, political, social, and religious, together with a statesmanlike account of the circumstances that led to the recent changes. Missions are not treated except incidentally, but the book is invaluable as setting forth the present-day problem of the most strategic of all Moslem lands.

DAVIS, RICHARD HARDING. The Congo and the Coasts of Africa. pp. 220. 1909 Scribner. $1.50

Impressions of the Congo country after a recent tour, written by a well-known correspondent and novelist; portrays the miserable condition of the Congo negro under the Leopold régime.

DU PLESSIS, J. A History of Christian Missions in South Africa. pp. 494. 1911. Longmans. 10s 6d.

An interesting and encyclopedic account of the missionary agencies at work in South Africa; gives an admirable survey of the whole work; makes a strong plea for closer co-operation and the organization of a national native Church.

FORBES, EDGAR ALLEN. The Land of the White Helmet. pp. 356. 1910. Revell. $1.50

Sketches by a well-known journalist relating to his recent tour in North and West Africa, touches on social, political and religious conditions

FRASER, DONALD. The Future of Africa. pp 309 1911. Y. P. M. M. London. 2s.

Treats of pagan Africa and mission work among the pagan races of Central and South Africa, written in the heart of the Dark Continent by one of the best-known missionaries to that country, and a former leader of the Student Christian Movement in Britain, as a text-book for mission study classes.

GAIRDNER, W. H. T. D. M. Thornton. pp. 283. 1909. Revell. $1.25

Well-written biography of a student leader in Britain who became a missionary leader in Egypt; accurate picture of work amongst Mohammedans at the educational center of the Moslem world.

GERDENER, G. B. A. Studies in the Evangelization of South Africa. pp. 211. 1911. Longmans. 2s 6d.

An analysis of the present missionary situation in South Africa, locating points of weakness in existing operations and calling for their readjustment on a statesmanlike basis.

GIFFEN, J KELLY. The Egyptian Sudan. pp. 252. 1905 Revell. $1.50.

Report of first three years' work of the Protestant pioneers in this section, first account of the land from actual residence there, full of information regarding a great military and economic center

HARRISON, MRS. J. W. Mackay of Uganda. pp. 488. 1900. Doran. $1.50.

Story of the remarkable life work of a civil engineer missionary who was a maker of Central Africa and who pioneered the work of what is now one of the most successful missions in the world.

HATTERSLEY, C. W. The Baganda at Home. pp. 227. 1909. Religious Tract Society. 5s.

A readable account of everyday life in the Uganda country.

HAWKER, GEORGE. An Englishwoman's Twenty-five Years in Tropical Africa. pp. 352. 1911. Hodder & Stoughton. 3s.

An account of the devoted work which Mrs. Lewis of the Baptist Missionary Society performed in the Cameroons and the Congo country.

HAWKER, GEORGE. The Life of George Grenfell. pp. 578. 1909. Revell $2.00

Life story of a distinguished Scotch missionary and statesman in the heart of Africa.

JACK, JAS. W. Daybreak in Livingstonia. pp. 371. 1900. Revell. $1 50.

One of the best discussions of missionary methods in Africa within a single volume; also gives the evolution of a most important mission

JOHNSTON, HARRY H. A History of the Colonization of Africa by Alien Races. pp. 349. 1905. The University Press.

Sir Harry Johnston writes from a long experience in Africa, as well as from much study of the subject; not missionary in character, but very important.

KUMM, H. KARL W. The Sudan. pp. 224. 1906. Marshall Bros. 3s. 6d.

Pictures a vast section of Africa with only sixteen missionaries and one of the most strategic areas in the missionary operations of to-day, shows the crisis occasioned by Moslem aggressions; well illustrated and full of information.

MACKENZIE, W. DOUGLAS. John Mackenzie. pp. 564. 1902 Doran. $2 00

The life story of a great South African missionary and statesman told by his son in great detail.

MACKINTOSH, C. W. Coillard of the Zambesi. pp. 484. 1907. American Tract Society. $2.50.

Account of the life of one of the greatest missionary statesmen of the twentieth century; stimulating story of self-denial and self-effacement; shows this missionary and his wife as empire-builders in South Africa.

MATTHEWS, T. T. Thirty Years in Madagascar. pp. 384. 1904. Doran. $1.75.

Out of thirty years' experience as a missionary, and after reading the records of earlier days in Madagascar, Mr. Matthews has been able to give a most authoritative and comprehensive account of a marvelous field and of the evolution of an interesting people.

MILLIGAN, ROBERT H The Jungle Folk of Africa. pp. 380. 1908 Revell. $1 50.

The outcome of seven years of missionary labor in the heart of the dark continent, the author is a keen observer and his descriptions are very vivid.

NASSAU, ROBERT H. Fetichism in West Africa. pp. 389. 1904. Scribner. $2.50

Forty years' observation of native customs and superstitions have enabled this missionary author to present a vast amount of material relating to every phase of the religious and social life of West Africa

NAYLOR, WILSON S. Daybreak in the Dark Continent. pp. 315. Revised 1912. Missionary Education Movement. 35 cents, 50 cents.

Text-book written for young people's classes after prolonged study of Africa and extensive journeys there, best brief and comprehensive survey

NOBLE, FREDERICK P. The Redemption of Africa. 2 vols. pp. 474; 391. 1899. Revell. $4.00

Though published over a decade ago, by far the best general work on Africa, viewed from the missionary standpoint; scholarly, of high literary merit, and intensely interesting, as well as encyclopedic.

PAGE, JESSE. The Black Bishop. pp. 440. 1909. Revell. $2.00.

Shows Samuel Adjai Crowther, the first negro Bishop of the Church of England, at work in the earlier years of the Niger Mission, which he founded; includes much information regarding the Nigerian peoples and the aggressions of Islam in that land.

STEWART, JAMES Dawn in the Dark Continent. pp. 400 1903. Revell. $2.00.

A story of missionary progress and methods, told by the greatest educator in South Africa, and one of the best authorities on the African continent, a briefer and less valuable contribution than Dr. Noble's book, but of great merit.

TREMEARNE, A. J N. The Niger and the West Sudan. pp 151 1910. Hodder & Stoughton. $2.00.

A vade mecum containing hints and suggestions for those who expect to travel or reside in West Africa, contains also historical and anthropological notes, written by a British army officer known also as an authority on this part of Africa.

TUCKER, A. R. Eighteen Years in Uganda and East Africa. 2 vols. pp. 359; 388. 1909. Arnold. 30s.

An account of Protestant Missions in Uganda, told by one who has been for many years a devoted missionary Bishop laboring there; contains the annals of a work which takes a front rank among the wonders of modern missions; optimistic, but founded on facts which justify an outlook of faith and hope.

VAN SOMMER, ANNIE, and ZWEMER, S. M., editors. Daylight in the Harem. pp. 224. 1911. Revell. $1.25.

A special volume reporting the papers read at the Lucknow Conference on Missions to Moslems, which related specially to the women of Islam; describes present-day reform movements, the conditions surrounding Moslem women and suitable methods of work among them.

WATSON, CHARLES R. In the Valley of the Nile. pp. 249. 1908. Revell. $1.00.

The best book extant on the work of missions in Egypt, written with sympathy and keen insight; tells both of results already attained and of problems yet unsolved.

WEEKS, JOHN H Congo Life and Folklore. pp. 468 1911 Religious Tract Society. 5s.

An interesting and valuable work in story form, bristling with information regarding Congo life, written by an experienced missionary who knows well the people and their folklore.

WELLS, JAMES Stewart of Lovedale pp 419. 1909 Revell. $1 50

A fascinating biography of one who was associated with Livingstone, and who originated Livingstonia, a companion volume to Dr. Stewart's "Dawn in the Dark Continent."

WHERRY, E. M, MYLREA, C G., and ZWEMER, S. M., editors. Lucknow, 1911 pp. 293 1911. Christian Literature Society for India Rupees 3.

A confidential report volume of the Second General Conference on Missions to Moslems, held at Lucknow, 1911; contains papers and a report of the discussions on the training of missionaries to Moslems and literature for Moslems; issued for private circulation only.

ZWEMER, SAMUEL M. Islam: A Challenge to Faith pp. 295. 1907. S. V M 35 cents, $1.00

Prepared as a text-book, but valuable also as a book of reference, and the best single volume for general reading on the religion which challenges Christianity for the religious conquest of Africa.

ASIA · VARIOUS COUNTRIES

BLAKESLEE, GEORGE H., editor. China and the Far East pp. 455. 1910 Crowell. $2 00

Lectures delivered during the second decennial celebration of the founding of Clark University, the various topics discussed by acknowledged experts, such as Chester Holcombe, I. W. Williams, Harlan P Beach, J W. Jenks, T F Millard, Hamilton Wright, Edward C. Moore, G T. Ladd, D Z Sheffield, Amos P Wilder.

CURTIS, LILLIAN JOHNSON. The Laos of North Siam. pp. 338. 1903 The Westminster Press. $1.25.

First full treatment of the little-known and most interesting Laos; written by one who traveled and labored among them for four years, account of mission work there; especially valuable for Presbyterians.

CURTIS, WILLIAM E. Around the Black Sea. pp. 456. 1911. Doran. $2.50.

Records the travels of a well-known journalist in Asia Minor; gives a vivid description of the conditions surrounding missionary life in the Near East.

CURTIS, WILLIAM E. Egypt, Burma, and British Malaysia. pp. 399. 1905. Revell. $2 00.

A well-known traveler and journalist gives the results of his observations in the countries named and in Hong Kong; Egypt and Burma especially good, though only a limited number of themes are discussed.

EDDY, GEORGE SHERWOOD. Japan and India. pp. 115. 1908. Indian National Council 15 cents.

Japan and its people described for educated Indians, more particularly the lessons which aspiring India may learn from progressive Japan; written by a prominent missionary in South India, after a visit to Japan

FLEESON, KATHARINE NEVILLE. Laos Folk-Lore of Farther India. pp. 153. 1899. Revell 75 cents.

Classified collection of tales, fables, riddles, parables and proverbs rendered into English by a sympathetic missionary as an interpretation of the Laos.

FOSTER, JOHN W. American Diplomacy in the Orient. pp. 498. 1903. Houghton, Mifflin. $3.00.

A most reliable and scholarly review, by an ex-Secretary of State, of America's relations with China, Japan, Korea, Hawaii, Samoa, and the Philippines, appreciative references to missionary work; excellent to furnish the background for a study of present conditions in these countries and of missionary work there

FREEMAN, JOHN H. An Oriental Land of the Free pp. 200. 1910. The Westminster Press. 35 cents, 50 cents.

A brief, interesting account of the Laos in Siam, Burma, China and Indo-China, and of mission work among them, written by one of the few missionaries to this little-known people

INGHAM, E GRAHAM From Japan to Jerusalem. pp. 232. 1911. London Church Missionary Society. 2s. 6d.

Missionary journey recently made by Bishop Ingham of the Church Missionary Society; deals chiefly with the work of that Society, but also discusses in a general way the present missionary opportunities in China, Japan, India and the Near East

KNOX, GEO. W. The Spirit of the Orient. pp. 312. 1906. Crowell. $1.50.

An interpretation of the spirit of the people of the Orient, first by contrast with the spirit of the West, and then by an examination in turn of the people and customs and the spirit and problems of India, China and Japan.

LITTLE, ARCHIBALD. The Far East. pp. 334. 1905. Clarendon Press. $2.00.

Deals mainly with the geographical and geological aspects of China, though Japan, Korea, and Siam are briefly described Best recent volume by one who has lived long in China and traveled widely.

MCKENZIE, F. A. The Unveiled East. pp 347. 1907. Dutton. $3.50.

A thorough, fair-minded treatment of present conditions in the Far East by a correspondent of the London *Daily Mail*, after extensive travels in Japan, China, and Korea, and personal experience in Kuroki's army. The author proves himself to be a strong friend of the missionary.

MILLARD, T. F. America and the Far Eastern Question. pp. 576. 1909. Moffat, Yard & Co. $4.00.

Interesting chapters on the new problems of the Orient, written with much frankness and from the standpoint of American interest; anti-Japanese in its treatment of Japan's international politics, written by an extensive traveler and close student of the Far Eastern question.

MONCRIEFF, G K. SCOTT. Eastern Missions from a Soldier's Standpoint. pp. 181. 1907. Religious Tract Society 58 cents

A British army captain's observations and conclusions regarding missionary work in India, China, Beluchistan, and on the Afghan border, a stout defense of missions.

MONTGOMERY, H. B. Western Women in Eastern Lands. pp. 286. 1911. Macmillan. 35 cents, 50 cents.

One of the series of text-books of the Central Committee of the United Study of Missions; excellent survey of woman's work for the women of non-Christian lands.

MOTT, JOHN R. Strategic Points in the World's Conquest. pp. 218. 1897. S. V. M. $1.00.

A report of the author's observations and deductions in the course of a tour made in 1905, including the great student centers of the world, informing and statesmanlike.

REINSCH, PAUL SAMUEL. Intellectual and Political Currents in the Far East. pp. 396. 1911. Houghton, Mifflin. $2.00

A strong and discriminating review of the present situation in the Orient, with special reference to the vast changes now in rapid progress; written by a diligent and well-equipped student of Far Eastern affairs.

SIAM AND LAOS AS SEEN BY OUR AMERICAN MISSIONARIES. pp. 552. 1884. Presbyterian Board of Publication. $1.50.

Collection of articles upon nearly every topic germane to a missionary volume, written by missionaries of the Presbyterian Board; old but useful.

SPEER, ROBERT E. Missions and Politics in Asia. pp. 271. 1898. Revell. $1.00.

Outcome of an extended tour in Asia in 1896-1897; although somewhat out of date regarding economic and political conditions in the Orient, still valuable for its revelation of the spirit of the peoples of the Far East and the part of Christian missions in the movements of progress and reform.

TOWNSEND, MEREDITH. Asia and Europe. pp. 404. 1910. Putnam. $2.50.

Most interesting essays on conditions and movements in the Nearer and Farther East, and the relation of Europe thereto; the outcome of a lifelong study of the relations between these two continents; some of the author's conclusions stated in the former edition of the book have since been strikingly verified.

WEALE, B. L. PUTNAM The Re-shaping of the Far East. 2 vols. pp. 548; 535 1905. Macmillan. $6.00.

Gives an understanding of some of the complex situations and problems in the Far East within recent years, discusses the Russo-Japanese war; prophesies intrigue and troubles succeeding the war, and emphasizes Great Britain's responsibilities in China.

ZWEMER, SAMUEL M., and BROWN, ARTHUR J. The Nearer and Farther East. pp. 325. 1908. Macmillan. 35 cents, 50 cents.

Studies dealing with Moslem lands and with Siam, Burma and Korea; arranged for women's church classes.

ARABIA, PERSIA AND THE LEVANT

ARPEE, LEON. The Armenian Awakening. pp. 235. 1909. University of Chicago Press. $1 25.

An account of the importance of the Armenian people, showing how, from their earliest history until the present time, they have been one of the leading races in Western Asia, and indicating the significance for them of the present reform movements

BARTON, JAMES L. Daybreak in Turkey pp. 296; cloth, pp. 306. 1908. Pilgrim Press. 50 cents, $1.50.

The best book on the Turkish Empire and the work of missions in that part of the world; scholarly and interesting.

BASMAJIAN, K. H. Life in the Orient. pp. 277. 1910. American Tract Society. $1.00.

An account of governmental and social conditions in the Ottoman Empire and of its every-day life; written from the standpoint of an earnest Armenian Christian; a revised edition covering the revolution and the rise of the Young Turk party

BUXTON, CHARLES R. Turkey in Revolution. pp. 285. 1909. Unwin. $2.50.

An interesting historical survey of recent years in Turkey and its neighboring States; a good supplement to Dr. Barton's book.

CURTIS, WILLIAM E. The Turk and His Lost Provinces. pp. 396. 1903. Revell $2.00.

Impressions of an American journalist concerning the Balkan Peninsula, less valuable than when written, but gives much readable information with respect to Constantinople and the "buffer States."

CURTIS, WILLIAM E. To-day in Syria and Palestine. pp. 529. 1903. Revell. $2.00.

An account of what an unusually keen and sympathetic observer deems of public interest. Recent history has confirmed some of his conclusions.

CURTIS, WILLIAM E. Turkestan, the Heart of Asia pp. 354. 1911. Doran $2 00.

A description from the pen of a careful journalist of a great unoccupied field; pictures vividly the chief cities, Bokhara, Khiva and Samarkand.

DOUGHTY, CHARLES M. Wanderings in Arabia. 2 vols. pp. 309; 297. 1908. Scribner. $4.50.

An abbreviated reprint of his earlier work, "Arabia Deserta," the most interesting account of Central and Western Asia, by one who is easily the greatest of all explorers in the neglected Peninsula, style fascinatingly archaic.

DWIGHT, HENRY O. Constantinople and Its Problems. pp. 298. 1901. Revell. $1.25.

Shows the relation of this world-capital to questions affecting Mohammedanism, Turkish womanhood, the Eastern Church problem, and the place of education in the uplift of the Empire; an able contribution to a right understanding of the subject.

FORDER, A. Ventures Among the Arabs. pp. 292. 1909 Gospel Publishing House. $1.00.

An interesting account of life among the Bedouin Arabs, by a free lance missionary who has shown great boldness in travel, although his work has not had permanent results.

GRIFFITH, MRS. M. E. HUME-. Behind the Veil in Persia and Turkish Arabia. pp. 336. 1909. Lippincott. $3 50.

Things as they are among Moslem women, by one who has loved them and lived among them; testimony which is an indictment of the present social system.

HAMLIN, CYRUS. My Life and Times. pp. 538. 1893. Revell. $1.50.

The life and missionary career of the maker of Robert College, a most versatile Yankee, whose life story is an inspiration.

JESSUP, HENRY HARRIS. Fifty-three Years in Syria 2 vols. pp. 404; 428. 1910. Revell. $5.00.

Valuable not only as an account of a noteworthy missionary who was a pioneer of Protestant missions in Syria, but as a history of missions in that land; gives an understanding of the changes now in progress in the Turkish Empire.

LEES, G. ROBINSON. The Witness of the Wilderness. pp. 222. 1909. Longmans $1.25.

LEES, G. ROBINSON. Village Life in Palestine. pp. 236. 1905 Longmans. $1.25.

Two books which give a description of the real home life, manners, customs, characteristics and superstitions of the peasants in Palestine and of the Bedouin tribes in North Arabia; the result of several years' residence and study on the ground.

LOTI, PIERRE. Disenchanted. pp. 381. 1908. Macmillan. $1 50.

A powerful novel with a purpose, shows that civilization without emancipation and the Gospel means spiritual loss for the women of Turkey.

MALCOLM, NAPIER. Five Years in a Persian Town. pp. 272. 1905. Dutton. $3.00

A sociological study of a typical town in Persia, valuable because of its minute character, and especially helpful to those who expect to enter this country.

RICHTER, JULIUS A History of Protestant Missions in the Near East. pp. 435. 1910. Revell. $2.50.

A thorough, scholarly and reliable account of the development of Protestant missions in Mohammedan lands, the standard volume on this subject, the English edition is more a revision for English and American readers than a translation from the German.

SINKER, ROBERT. Memorials of the Hon Ion Keith-Falconer. pp. 258. 1903. Deighton, Bell & Co. $1 85

The best biography of this pioneer missionary to Arabia, quoting largely from his own letters and addresses.

VAN SOMMER, ANNIE, and ZWEMER, SAMUEL M., editors. Our Moslem Sisters pp. 299 1907. Revell. $1.25.

Chiefly papers prepared for the Cairo Conference, 1906; affords a striking and faithful picture of the social and domestic conditions affecting the women of Moslem countries.

WASHBURN, GEORGE. Fifty Years in Constantinople. pp. 316. 1910. Houghton, Mifflin. $3 00

Largely a history of Robert College, but incidentally gives first-hand information of social and political events of great interest in Turkish history.

WILSON, S. G. Persian Life and Customs. pp. 333 1895. Revell. $1.25.

Written after fifteen years of missionary service; covers the field very satisfactorily.

WISHARD, J. G. Twenty Years in Persia. pp. 349. 1908. Revell. $1.50.

More than a handbook on Iran, gives an account of missionary conditions, and paints the background of the transformations now taking place in that country; suggests the opportunities for medical mission work there.

ZWEMER, SAMUEL M. Arabia: The Cradle of Islam. pp. 434. 1900. Revell. $2.00.

The best book by far on Arabia and missions there, valuable also for missionaries to other Moslem lands.

CHINA

BALL, J DYER. Things Chinese. pp. 816. 1904. Scribner. $4.00.

Thesaurus of information on Chinese affairs; arranged in alphabetical order; written by one who has *spent forty years in China, in a style that is readable* and not encyclopedic, very valuable.

BALL, J. DYER. The Chinese at Home. pp. 369. 1911. Revell. $2.00.

An interesting study of the Chinese, their manners and character, social customs and religious beliefs; includes an account of missionary work and its results.

BARBER, W. T. A. David Hill, Missionary and Saint. pp. 337. 1898. Kelly. 3s. 6d.

The best life of an eminent evangelistic missionary of Central China, whose godliness impressed alike foreigners and Chinese, Pastor Hsi in particular.

BEACH, HARLAN P. Dawn on the Hills of T'ang. pp. 227. 1905. S. V. M. 35 cents, 50 cents.

Concise summary of pertinent facts about China and mission work there; a valuable feature is its pronouncing vocabulary of Chinese names and stations, with indications of the societies laboring in them and the force employed.

BLAKESLEE, GEORGE H., editor. China and the Far East. pp. 455. 1910. Crowell. $2.00.

Gives an excellent survey of present conditions in the Far East and indicates China's relation thereto; a collection of lectures delivered at Clark University during the second decennial celebration by prominent authorities on Far Eastern questions; only live topics are treated.

BLAND, J. O. P., and BACKHOUSE, E. China Under the Empress Dowager. pp. 525. 1910. Lippincott. 16s.

A striking and timely historical sketch of the life and times of Tzu Hsi; gives glimpses back of the scenes in the troublous days of the Boxer Uprising; a record founded on the diary of Ching Shan.

BROOMHALL, MARSHALL. Present Day Conditions in China. pp. 58. 1909. China Inland Mission. 50 cents.

Indicates the remarkable changes and progress of recent years in China; striking charts and statistics.

BROOMHALL, MARSHALL, editor. The Chinese Empire. pp. 450. 1907. Morgan & Scott. $2.50.

A symposium on the Chinese Empire, each of the nineteen provinces being treated by a separate writer, together with a number of special papers; indices; of more than usual reference value.

BROOMHALL, MARSHALL. Islam in China. pp. 332. 1910. China Inland Mission. 7s 6d.

The first book on this subject in the English language, is at once an historical account and an analysis of present-day conditions; based on thorough investigation and ripe scholarship; written by a missionary authority who by his experience in China and his investigations for the World Missionary Conference has had excellent opportunities to study the question exhaustively; valuable for all students of China and the Chinese.

BURTON, MARGARET E. The Education of Women in China. pp. 232 1911. Revell. $1.25.

A scholarly and interesting account of the development and present status of the education of Chinese women; gives a statesmanlike summons to enlarged activities in this direction; conclusions drawn from first-hand observation and diligent study.

BROWN, ARTHUR J. New Forces in Old China. pp. 382. 1904. Revell. $1.50.

Unusually accurate and valuable account of Old China and its people; review of the commercial, economic, political, and missionary forces that are aiding in its transformation; and a forecast of the future of the Empire

BROWN, ARTHUR J The Chinese Revolution. pp. 217. 1912. S. V. M. 50 cents; 75 cents.

An illuminating review of the present situation in China, treats of the economic, social, educational and religious changes which are ushering in China's new day; written as a text-book for students.

CECIL, WILLIAM GASCOYNE-. Changing China. pp. 342. 1910. Appleton. $3.00.

An account of the new developments in China, as seen by Lord Cecil in his visits to that country in 1907 and 1909, with a thoughtful study of their causes.

CLARKE, SAMUEL R. Among the Tribes in Southwest China. pp. 315. 1911. China Inland Mission. 3s. 6d.

An original contribution to the study of the aboriginal people of China; contains a striking account of the conversion of the Miao, Shan and other tribes.

CONGER, MRS. E. H. Letters from China. pp. 391. 1909 McClurg. $2.75.

Informal and most interesting letters by the wife of a well-known diplomatist, who had unusual opportunities to gather information about the lives and customs of the Chinese, and especially of Chinese women, from the late Empress Dowager down; includes experience of the beleaguered at Peking; many appreciative references to missionary work in China.

DEGROOT, J. J. M. The Religion of the Chinese. pp. 230 1910. Macmillan. $1.25.

The latest of many books on this subject by the same author; a readable and scholarly account of the religious beliefs of China—Animism, Confucianism, Taoism, and Buddhism, by a foremost authority; valuable to an understanding of the Chinese people.

GEIL, WILLIAM EDGAR. Eighteen Capitals of China. pp. 429. 1911. Lippincott. $5.00.

A delightful description of present-day life in the great centers of China, written by a well-known traveler.

GIBSON, J. CAMPBELL. Mission Problems and Mission Methods in South China. pp. 334. 1901. Revell. $1.50.

One of the best volumes on the subject treated; takes the reader into the heart of the missionary's problems, beginning with the religious and literary background and proceeding to the full-fledged church and its external relations.

GILMOUR, JAMES Among the Mongols. pp. 383. Revell. $1.25.

A Robinson Crusoe style of book, which is unequalled for vividness and warmth of Christian interest. The reader lives in Mongol tents, rides Mongol horses and watches the canny Scot as he tirelessly lives and preaches Christ.

GRIFFIS, W. E. China's Story. pp. 302. 1911. Houghton, Mifflin. $1.25.

An historical sketch of the Chinese; an interpretation presented from their own viewpoint as seen in their art and literature rather than as judged by the foreigner; gives evidence of scholarship and research, yet written in an attractive style; written by a well-known student of the life and peoples of the Far East.

HEADLAND, ISAAC T. Court Life in China. pp. 372. 1909. Revell. $1.50.

Interesting sketches of the late Empress Dowager, also of members of the Imperial family and ladies of rank, with a description of the social life of the higher classes; written by a keen observer who has had a rare opportunity to observe.

HOLCOMBE, CHESTER. The Real Chinaman. pp. 350. 1909. Dodd, Mead & Co. $2.00.

Removes many misunderstandings regarding the Chinaman as he is; written by a sympathetic and unbiased diplomat.

HUNT, WILLIAM R. Heathenism Under the Searchlight. pp. 153. 1911. American Tract Society 50 cents.

A missionary's unsparing statement of the impotence of the religions of China to direct and bless her at this hour of her crisis.

MACGILLIVRAY, D., editor. A Century of Protestant Missions in China. pp. 677. 1907. American Presbyterian Mission. $3.00.

Contains a mass of most valuable statistics and important facts on China showing the results of missionary work in the Empire and the extent of present operations; a reliable and important book of reference.

MACGILLIVRAY, D., editor. The China Mission Year Book. pp. 567. 1911. Missionary Education Movement. $1.50.

Contains reliable information on present conditions in China, and presents the recent progress of the missionary movement; devotes special attention to the higher and educated classes of the Chinese; excellent appendices, statistical table, and a directory of missionaries in China.

MCNABB, R. L. The Women of the Middle Kingdom. pp. 160. 1903. Jennings & Graham. 75 cents.

Contains information regarding many phases of girlhood and womanhood in China, dwells on their religious needs and the efforts made to meet them.

MARTIN, W. A. P. The Awakening of China. pp. 328. 1907. Doubleday, Page & Co. $3.80

A readable volume dealing with the provinces and outlying territories of China, the history of the Empire and the recent changes that have been taking place, written by a former president of the Chinese Imperial University

MERWIN, SAMUEL. Drugging a Nation. pp. 212. 1908. Revell. $1 00.

A faithful story of the opium curse of China.

MINER, LUELLA. China's Book of Martyrs. pp. 512. 1903. Westminster Press. $1.50.

Fullest work on the Chinese martyrs of the Boxer Uprising of 1900; largely in the words of witnesses and friends of the slain; deeply moving and often horrible.

MOULE, ARTHUR EVANS. Half a Century in China. pp. 343. 1911. Doran. $2.00.

Pictures strikingly the contrast between the old order and the new in China; interprets the changing conditions there and indicates the service which Christian missionary effort can render to China in this transitional time; written after fifty years' experience by Venerable Archdeacon Moule, one of the best students and most valued servants of China.

OSGOOD, ELLIOTT I. Breaking Down Chinese Walls. pp. 217. 1908. Revell. $1 00.

Written out of extended hospital experience in China, a practical proof of the value as well as the need of medical missions.

PARKER, E. H. China; Her History, Diplomacy and Commerce. pp. 332. 1901. Dutton. $2.50.

Based mainly upon Chinese records and a quarter century's personal acquaintance with China, this volume is of the greatest value; the scope is broader than the title suggests, including geography, population, army, rebellions, religion, national characteristics, calendar, etc.

ROSS, E. A. The Changing Chinese. pp. 356. 1911. Century Company. $2.40.

A really indispensable book to one who wishes to understand the China of to-day; economic, social, educational and religious aspects of the situation are discussed after a study on the ground by one of the leading sociological authorities of the day; a keen and reliable treatise most interestingly written and well illustrated.

SMITH, ARTHUR H. Village Life in China. pp. 360. 1899. Revell. $2.00.

Informal sociological studies of the North China village, its institutions, usages, public characters, and family life, with chapter on Christianity's task in its regeneration.

SMITH, ARTHUR H. China and America To-day. pp. 256. 1907. Revell. $1.25.

A review of the relation between the United States and China, showing China's grounds both for grievance and gratitude; gives a more favorable impression of the Chinaman than the author's "Chinese Characteristics"; a plea for fairness and consideration.

SMITH, ARTHUR H. The Uplift of China. pp. 274. Revised 1912 Missionary Education Movement. 35 cents, 50 cents.

A text-book for young people's classes, presenting a brief outline of progress in China and the development of missionary work there, with a sufficient background dealing with the country and people.

SMITH, ARTHUR H. China in Convulsion. 2 vols. pp. 364; 406. 1901. Revell. $5 00.

The standard work on the Boxer uprising and massacres of 1900, by one who was himself in the siege at Peking.

SOOTHILL, W. E. A Typical Mission in China. pp. 293 1907. Revell. $1.50.

Justifies its title; describes typical Chinese, typical experiences, typical methods of work, a few chapters devoted to the native and foreign religions of China.

STANFORD, E. S. Atlas of the Chinese Empire. 1909. China Inland Mission. $4.00.

An excellent atlas, designed especially to accompany Broomhall's "The Chinese Empire", accuracy and clearness are features.

TAYLOR, MRS. HOWARD. Pastor Hsi: Confucian Scholar and Christian. pp. 494. 1907. China Inland Mission. $1.50.

A striking illustration of the divine power working in missions in China, describing the conversion of a Chinese scholar; combines in one volume Mrs. Taylor's two previous narratives about Mr. Hsi.

THOMPSON, RALPH WARDLAW. Griffith John. pp. 544. 1906. Doran. $2.00

The story of the life and labor and love of one of the great figures in missionary history, one who learned to know the real Chinaman intimately.

TOWNSEND, WILLIAM JOHN. Robert Morrison, Pioneer of Chinese Missions. pp. 160. 1902. Revell. 75 cents.

Useful sketch of a great pioneer, the centennial of whose arrival was celebrated in China in 1907.

WALSHE, GILBERT W. Ways that Are Dark. pp. 276. 1907. Kelley & Walsh. $1.50.

Unexcelled chapters on "Chinese Etiquette and Social Procedure," written by one who knew whereof he wrote; made clear by half-tones and diagrams; invaluable for missionaries desiring to become personæ gratæ to the Chinese, especially of the higher classes.

WEALE, B. L. PUTNAM. The Coming Struggle in Eastern Asia pp 656. 1908. Macmillan. $3.50.

The last in a series of four works by this author dealing with the Far Eastern problem, critical of Japan; Part III examines the remarkable changes of late years in China and the relation thereto of American interests.

WILLIAMS, MRS. ISABELLA B. By the Great Wall. pp. 400. 1909 Revell. $1.50.

Selected correspondence of a devoted and highly-equipped missionary of the American Board in North China.

WILLIAMS, S. WELLS. The Middle Kingdom. 2 vols. pp. 836; 775. 1883. Scribner. $9.00

Still remains by far the most valuable general work on China, written by America's foremost Sinologue; encyclopedic, though not so in form.

INDIA AND CEYLON

ANDERSON, WILLIAM B, and WATSON, CHARLES R. Far North in India. pp. 312. 1911. Board of Foreign Missions of the United Presbyterian Church of North America. 50 cents.

While dealing specially with the United Presbyterian Missions in the Punjab, gives valuable information regarding the needs and problems of all missionary work in that part of India.

AZARIAH, V S. India and Missions pp. 109. 1909. Christian Literature Society for India. 4 annas

A brief text-book written for Indian Christians by one of the most distinguished of their leaders, packed with trustworthy information.

BARRY, A. England's Mission to India. 1894. S. P. C. K 3s.

A wise and thorough exposition, chiefly from the viewpoint of a Churchman, of England's duty and responsibility to India, deals not simply with the religious obligations, but with the political, educational, and social aspects of a great trust.

BEACH, HARLAN P. India and Christian Opportunity pp. 308. 1908. S. V. M. 35 cents, 50 cents.

No small book can be named which will give the wide range of information about India which is supplied here; an unusually full study class text-book.

BUNKER, ALONZO. Soo Thah; A Tale of the Making of the Karen Nation. pp. 280 1902. Revell. $1.00.

True story by a veteran missionary to Burma, giving a graphic view of the daily life of heathen Hillmen, the entrance of the Gospel, and its transforming results.

CARMICHAEL, AMY WILSON-. Things as They Are Mission Work in Southern India. pp. 303. 1906. Revell. $1.00.

The strongest piece of realistic writing in Indian missionary literature; illustrations and subscripts most unusual; depressing because only the darkest side is portrayed.

CARMICHAEL, AMY WILSON- Overweight of Joy. pp. 300. 1906. Revell. $1.00.

The other side of the shield; as realistic as the preceding book, but incidents are chosen to reveal the Gospel's supernatural power; excellent illustrations.

CHAMBERLAIN, JACOB The Kingdom in India. pp. 301. 1908. Revell. $1.50.

Practically an autobiography of a great missionary veteran, vivid descriptions of missionary life and work in India.

COCHRANE, HENRY P. Among the Burmans. pp. 281. 1904. Revell. $1.25.

Gives a true picture of Burmese religions, superstitions and customs, as seen in the common life. Missionary work is clearly and encouragingly described.

CURTIS, WILLIAM E. Modern India. pp. 503. 1905 Revell. $2.00.

A keen and careful journalist's letters concerning his travels; gives a general knowledge of the Empire; little said about missions, though the author is sympathetic.

DATTA, SURENDRA K. The Desire of India. pp. 307. 1908. Student Volunteer Missionary Union. $1 00. Missionary Education Movement. 35 cents, 50 cents.

One of the best brief works on India and missionary work there, has the advantage of the sympathetic insight of its Indian authorship, used widely as a text-book by the students of Great Britain.

DYER, HELEN S. Pandita Ramabai. pp. 197. Revised 1911. Revell. $1.25.

Best life of this talented Indian woman; account of her successful efforts in behalf of the widows of India.

DYER, HELEN S. Revival in India. pp. 158. 1907. Gospel Publishing House 50 cents.

Typical and authentic incidents of the recent spiritual awakening in India.

EDDY, GEORGE SHERWOOD. India Awakening. pp. 257. 1911. Missionary Education Movement. 35 cents, 50 cents.

Not a thorough-going treatise on India, but a series of reliable and interesting sketches of present-day life there, viewed from the missionary's standpoint; vivid, thoroughly up-to-date, sparkling with information and frequently anecdotal; written as a text-book for classes by a well-known missionary leader in India.

FARQUHAR, J. N. A Primer of Hinduism. pp. 187. 1911. Christian Literature Society for India. 4 annas.

A masterly survey of the great religion of India; treats it as a unit and traces its development through the various stages of its history; valuable to an understanding of the hearts and homes of the Hindus of to-day; excellent bibliography and numerous illustrations; written by one of the most scholarly and sympathetic students of Hinduism

FRASER, ANDREW H. L. Among India's Rajahs and Ryots. pp. 368. 1911. Lippincott. $4.00.

A book of merit and unusual interest; throws light upon numerous phases of life in India; relates many of the personal experiences, and reflects the mature judgments upon political and missionary affairs, of an illustrious British administrator, recently Lieutenant-Governor of Bengal, who for thirty-seven years in the British civil service was a true friend of the Indians and a loyal supporter of missionary effort.

FRAZER, ROBERT WATSON. British India. pp. 399. 1897. Putnam. $1.50.

A summary of the history of British India, in the well-known series of "Stories of the Nations."

FULLER, MRS. MARCUS B The Wrongs of Indian Womanhood. pp. 302. 1900. Revell. $1.25.

Description and discussion of these wrongs in the desire to find a missionary remedy

GRIFFIN, Z. F. Chundra Lela. pp. 84. 1911. Griffin & Rowland Press. 50 cents.

The story of a Hindu devotee and Christian missionary.

HACKER, I. H. A Hundred Years in Travancore. pp. 106. 1908. Allenson. 2s. 6d.

The centenary memorial volume of the work of the London Missionary Society in Travancore, affords an excellent idea of the nature, scope and evolution of mission work in South India.

HOLCOMB, HELEN H. Men of Might in India Missions. pp 352. 1901 Revell. $1 25.

Lives of thirteen famous missionaries of various nationalities, ranging from the first Protestant missionary to Dr. Kellogg, who died in 1899; selection is good, emphasis satisfactory, and treatment fairly full.

HUME, ROBERT A. An Interpretation of India's Religious History. pp. 224. 1911. Revell. $1 25.

A thoughtful, although popular, study of the earlier and later religious history of India, and especially of those elements in it which have been preparing the way for Christianity; written from a sympathetic viewpoint by one of the best-known missionaries to that country.

HUME, ROBERT A. Missions from the Modern View. pp. 292. 1905. Revell. $1 25.

Lectures by a well-known missionary at Ahmednagar on certain phases of the science of missions; discusses the modern view of God and the world, the relation of missions to sociology and psychology, the points of contact between Christianity and Hinduism, and the spirit in which the Gospel should be presented to Hindus.

HUNTER, WILLIAM W. The Indian Empire: Its Peoples, History, and Products. Map, Tables. pp. 852. 1893. Smith, Elder & Co. 21s.

Encyclopedic account of historical and present-day India from the standpoint of a civilian; most authoritative single volume on the Empire, considering its scope.

HUNTER, WILLIAM W. A Brief History of the Indian Peoples. pp. 256. 1897. Clarendon Press. 90 cents.

Sir William Hunter is the highest authority on India, and this volume is a condensation of fuller works by the same author, especially the one named above; used in civil service examinations by the British Government.

JONES, JOHN P. India's Problem, Krishna or Christ. pp. 381. 1903. Revell. $1 50.

Except for the first chapter, the book is wholly devoted to the Indian religions, womanhood of India, and a full discussion of missions in their methods and problems; extremely valuable.

JONES, JOHN P. India: Its Life and Thought. pp. 448. 1908. Macmillan. $2 50.

A recent book by a well-known missionary who is one of the sanest and strongest thinkers on Indian problems; gives in readable form an account of the faiths of India and the present religious movements in the Empire; not a repetition of the preceding book.

LUCAS, BERNARD. The Empire of Christ. pp. 151. 1907. Macmillan. 80 cents.

An examination of present missionary methods and objectives; throws the emphasis strongly on the Gospel's mission to pervade and transform society as distinguished from the gaining of individual converts; will appeal to thinkers of the liberal school; written by an experienced missionary in India.

MACDONELL, ARTHUR A. A History of Sanskrit Literature. pp. 472. 1900. Appleton. $1.50

First history of Sanskrit literature as a whole; necessarily brief in its treatment, which is supplemented by the bibliographical notes appended to the book; indispensable to a thorough understanding of India.

MASON, CAROLINE A. The Little Green God. pp. 146. 1902. Revell. 75 cents.

A powerful setting forth of the harm done by church women in society through patronizing Swamis and living merely for selfish ends, incidentally a fine defense of the underestimated missionary on furlough.

MAXWELL, ELLEN B. The Bishop's Conversion pp. 384. 1892. Eaton & Mains. $1.50

Under the guise of fiction this former missionary gives an intimate and true account of the real missionary life, with the object of furnishing an answer to critics of Indian missions, not especially strong as a novel

MORRISON, JOHN. New Ideas in India. pp. 282. 1907. Macmillan. $1.60.

A discerning examination of the social and religious trends in India during the past century, and especially the past decade; a thoughtful, reliable book, written by an experienced missionary educator in Calcutta.

MURDOCH, J. Sketches of Indian Christians. pp 257. 1896. The Christian Literature Society for India. 2s.

Brief accounts from various sources of the lives of some distinguished Indian Christians, both men and women, with an introduction by the late Professor S. Satthianadhan, of the Presidency College, Madras.

MYLNE, LOUIS GEORGE. Missions to Hindus. pp 189. 1908. Longmans. $1.20.

A study by the Bishop of Bombay of missionary methods in India; includes a discussion of caste, Hindu theology, Hindu character, and the results of missions; of special value to missionaries to India.

PURSER, W. C. B. Christian Missions in Burma. pp. 246. 1911. Doran. $2.00.

A brief sketch of the history, beliefs and every-day life of the Burmese people, followed by an account of the work done among them by the Roman Catholics, the Baptists and the S. P. G.

RICHTER, JULIUS. A History of Protestant Missions in India. pp. 468. 1908. Revell. $2.50.

An excellent translation of "Indische Missions Geschichte"; clear and away the best book on Christian missions to India; scholarly and comprehensive; the first part historical, while the second part deals with the problems, organization, results, and outlook of Indian missions; written by one of the world's great missionary authorities.

ROBINSON, WILLIAM. By Temple Shrine and Lotus Pool. pp. 296. 1910. Morgan & Scott. 6s

Striking, well-written sketches of missionary work in India; gives a vivid portrayal of caste and the spiritual needs of that land, discusses missionary problems and methods of work.

RUSSELL, NORMAN. Village Work in India. pp. 251. 1902. Revell. $1.00.

Pen-pictures from a Canadian missionary's experience in Central India. Despite fanciful titles and wearisome interweaving of native words and phrases, it is very forceful.

SMITH, GEORGE. The Life of William Carey, D D. pp. 389. 1887. John Murray. 7s. 6d.

SMITH, GEORGE. The Life of Alexander Duff, D. D., LL. D. pp. 382. 1900. Hodder & Stoughton. Out of print.

These two lives—one of the English pioneer, the other of Scotland's most famous educational missionary and secretary—are classics. Dr. Duff's life is condensed from an earlier two-volume edition.

SORABJI, CORNELIA. Between the Twilights. pp. 191. 1908. Harper (London). 5s.

Sketches written by a brilliant East Indian woman, giving a vivid portrayal of the conditions in which her countrywomen are living.

WHERRY, E. M. Islam and Christianity in India and the Far East. pp. 238. 1907. Revell. $1.25.

Descriptive of the conditions, problems, and successes of missionary work among Mohammedans in the Orient, but particularly in India; written out of thirty years' missionary experience in that country.

JAPAN

ASHTON, W. G. A History of Japanese Literature. pp. 408. 1901. Appleton. $1.50.

Best summary of twelve centuries of Japanese literature; by one of the highest English authorities; invaluable for missionaries to Japan.

BACON, ALICE MABEL. Japanese Girls and Women. pp. 333. 1891. Houghton, Mifflin. $1.25.

Written by one who for years had the best opportunities of studying her subjects on the ground; gives an excellent view of all phases of the subject, especially of the life of women of the higher classes.

BATCHELOR, JOHN. The Ainu of Japan. pp. 336. Revell. Out of print.

The best book on the interesting aborigines of Northern Japan by the best-known missionary among them.

CARY, OTIS. Japan and Its Regeneration. pp. 150. Revised 1908. S. V. M. 35 cents, 50 cents.

Excellent, brief account of Japan and of missions there, written by a recognized missionary scholar; best text-book for study classes; well arranged for student use; statistics.

CARY, OTIS. A History of Christianity in Japan. 2 vols. pp. 367; 431. 1909. Revell. $2.50 each.

The best single work on missions in Japan; Volume I deals with Roman Catholic and Greek orthodox missions; Volume II with Protestant missions; gives evidence of scholarship and accurate knowledge, statistics recent and reliable; the standard work on the subject.

CHAMBERLAIN, BASIL HALL. Things Japanese. pp. 545. 1902. John Murray, London. $4.00.

Professor Chamberlain is the foremost English authority on Japan. The subjects are arranged in alphabetical order, with full index of less important items.

CLEMENT, ERNEST W. Christianity in Modern Japan. pp. 205. 1905. American Baptist Publication Society. $1.00.

Gives a bird's-eye view of the work of Christianity, especially since 1858; includes Roman and Greek Catholic work and that of the various Protestant societies, the work of auxiliary agencies, etc.

CLEMENT, ERNEST W. A Handbook of Modern Japan. pp. 395. 1905. McClurg. $1.40.

Just what its title indicates, and written by a missionary educator of Tokio; later than Professor Chamberlain's work and fuller on missions.

DEFOREST, JOHN H. Sunrise in the Sunrise Kingdom. pp. 233. 1909. Missionary Education Movement. 35 cents, 50 cents.

Brief and interesting text-book, intended primarily for church young people's classes; useful statistics

GREENE, D. C., and FISHER, G. M., editors. The Christian Movement in Japan. pp. 599. 1911. Missionary Education Movement. 90 cents.

A carefully prepared volume of recent information regarding the missionary operations in Japan, with a sketch of present conditions in that country; valuable appendices, statistics, and directory of missionaries in Japan

GRIFFIS, WILLIAM E Verbeck of Japan. pp. 376. 1900. Revell $1.50.

Life and work of the most influential missionary and publicist that Japan has had; described by one who knew him and his work very well.

GRIFFIS, WILLIAM E. A Maker of the New Orient. pp. 332. 1902. Revell. $1.25.

An appreciative story of the life and work of Samuel Robbins Brown, pioneer educator in China and Japan.

GRIFFIS, WILLIAM E. The Religions of Japan. pp. 457. 1895. Scribner. $2.00.

A brief, careful outline, by one of Japan's most faithful interpreters, of nature worship, Shintoism, Confucianism, and Buddhism, with a chapter on Roman Christianity in Japan in the seventeenth century.

GRIFFIS, WILLIAM E. The Mikado's Empire. 2 vols. pp. 324; 353. 1906. Harper. $4.00.

Eleventh edition of the standard American work on Japan and one of the best published; encyclopedic in its range, brought down to date from 1876 by appended chapters.

GULICK, SIDNEY L. Evolution of the Japanese. pp. 463. 1905. Revell. $2.00.

Incomparably the best exposition of Japan's evolution and national character, as well as of its people, that has been published in any western tongue.

HARDY, ARTHUR S. Life and Letters of Joseph Hardy Neesima. pp. 350. 1891. Houghton, Mifflin. $2.00.

The most satisfactory life of Japan's foremost Christian educator; written by the son of Neesima's American benefactor.

KNOX, GEORGE W. The Development of Religion in Japan. pp. 204. 1907. Putnam. $1.50.

An interesting history of the evolution of barbaric tribes into one of the world's foremost nations; describes the successive religions that have been introduced into the islands; written by a former missionary to that country

LAMPE, W. E. The Japanese Social Organization. pp. 84. 1910. Princeton University Press. 50 cents.

A treatise dealing with the fundamental characteristics of the Japanese social structure; indicates the elements of essential strength and weakness in the social organization of Japan.

LLOYD, ARTHUR. Everyday Japan. pp. 381. 1909 Cassell. $4.00

Interesting sketches written by an educator after twenty-five years' experience in Japan; full of information regarding the daily life of the people, beautifully illustrated.

MACKAY, GEORGE L. From Far Formosa. pp. 346. 1895. Revell. $1.25.

Occasionally prosy, yet for the most part an extremely interesting account of the achievements and thrilling experiences of Canada's missionary hero, a most fruitful life

MOODY, CAMPBELL N. The Heathen Heart. pp. 250. 1907. Oliphant. 3s. 6d.

Story of missions among the Chinese of Formosa; illustrates missionary experiences and methods of work among animistic peoples; relates wonderful triumphs of the Gospel.

KOREA

ALLEN, HORACE N. Things Korean. pp. 256. 1908 Revell. $1.25.

Informing and entertaining; written in discursive style by one who pioneered medical missions in Korea, and has since been a distinguished diplomatist.

BAIRD, ANNIE L. A. Daybreak in Korea. pp. 123 1909. Revell. 60 cents

A simple narrative likely to awaken interest in the uninterested; written from the Korean viewpoint; depicts faithfully the life of this most interesting people, especially the life of Korean women.

BISHOP, ISABELLA BIRD. Korea and Her Neighbors pp. 488. 1897. Revell. $2.00.

Based on four visits of an experienced world-traveler, mainly a record of journeying, but with encyclopedic information inserted, which is made available by a full index, missionary testimony indirect, but valuable.

DAVIS, G. T. B. Korea for Christ. pp. 68. 1910. Revell. 25 cents.

Interesting sketches relating to the remarkable religious revival now in progress in Korea; written by a missionary to that country.

FENWICK, MALCOLM C. The Church of Christ in Korea. pp. 134. 1911. Doran. $1.00.

Reveals, by way of an autobiographical missionary record covering twenty years, the situation in the Korean Church at the present time; justly magnifies the importance of working through native agents.

GALE, JAMES S. Korean Sketches. pp. 256. 1898. Revell. $1.00.

A most readable volume on Korea and trustworthy withal. Missions are only slightly dealt with, the people and their daily environment are the themes.

GALE, JAMES S. The Vanguard: A Tale of Korea. pp. 320. 1904. Revell. $1.50.

The story, thinly disguised by fiction, of actual Korean missionaries and Christians, with the old and new life in strong and interesting contrasts, one of the best missionary stories

GALE, JAMES S. Korea in Transition. pp. 270. 1909. Missionary Education Movement. 35 cents, 50 cents.

The best text-book on Korea for study classes, portrays vividly missionary life and work there.

HURLBERT, HOMER. The Passing of Korea. pp. 473 1906. Doubleday, Page. $3.80.

A voluminous and highly interesting series of sketches covering the history, institutions, every-day life, and political fortunes of Korea; extremely friendly to Korea and severely critical of Japan.

LONGFORD, JOSEPH H. The Story of Korea. pp. 400. 1911. Unwin. 10s. 6d.

A valuable account of Korea, past and present, by a former British Consul at Nagasaki; refers at length to the earlier Roman Catholic Missions and briefly to the modern missions.

MCKENZIE, F. A. The Tragedy of Korea. pp. 312. 1908. Dutton. $2.00.

A readable and illuminating statement of the present political situation in Korea, presents Korea's case in the matter of the Japanese occupation; by a well-known British war correspondent.

NOBLE, W. ARTHUR. Ewa: A Tale of Korea pp. 354. 1906. Eaton & Mains. $1.25.

In the guise of fiction, gives some interesting information about Korean customs and reveals native criticisms of foreigners.

UNDERWOOD, HORACE G. The Call of Korea. pp 204. 1908. Revell. 35 cents, 75 cents.

Reveals Korea's supreme need of the Gospel at the present hour, and her remarkable responsiveness; full of information, written by one of the best-known missionaries to that country.

UNDERWOOD, MRS. L. H. Fifteen Years Among the Top-Knots. pp. 271. 1904. American Tract Society. $1.50

While dealing largely with the author's own work as a Presbyterian medical missionary, the book includes other missions and workers as well; contains records of journeys, sometimes adventurous, peeps into the homes, sketches of Christians, inside views of the palace life, etc.

LATIN AMERICA

BEACH, HARLAN P. Protestant Missions in South America. pp. 236. 1907. S. V. M. 50 cents.

The only volume treating of missions in detail throughout the continent; intended primarily for student mission study classes.

BROWN, HUBERT W Latin America. pp. 308. 1901. Revell. $1.20.

General account of religious conditions in the republics south of the United States. Papists, patriots, Protestants, and mission problems are discussed, as well as the pagan background.

BUTLER, WILLIAM. Mexico in Transition. pp. 324. 1892. Western Methodist Book Concern. $2.00.

As a faithful description of conditions at the time and a historical sketch up to the time it was written, the book still has value

CLARK, FRANCIS E. The Continent of Opportunity. pp 350. 1907. Revell. $1.50.

Impressions of the South American republics, gained from extensive travels in that continent; presents data to justify the book's title, from the standpoint of Christian missions; written by the President of the World's Christian Endeavor Union.

CLARK, FRANCIS E., and HARRIET A. The Gospel in Latin Lands. pp. 315. 1909. Macmillan. 35 cents, 50 cents.

A sketchy account of Protestant work in the Latin countries of Europe and America; written by authors who have traveled widely and observed well; a text-book for women's classes.

DENIS. PIERRE. Brazil. Translated by Bernard Miall. pp. 388. 1911. Scribner. $3.00.

A most informing discussion of a vast and interesting country conducted from a great variety of viewpoints, the latest volume in the South American Series.

ENOCK, C. REGINALD. Peru. pp. 305. 1910. Scribner $3 00.

Gives a vivid impression of the resources and growing prosperity of this republic, together with an historical survey.

ENOCK, C. REGINALD. Mexico. pp. 356. 1910 Scribner. $3 00.

An account of the ancient and modern civilization of this land of absorbing interest; describes vividly the economic and political conditions furnishing a background of knowledge against which the developments of the present day are more clearly understood.

GRUBB, W. BARBROOKE. Among the Indians of the Paraguayan Chaco. pp. 176. 1904. South American Missionary Society. 1s. 6d.

The author and his fellow-workers describe interestingly the environments, habits, character, language and arts of the Chaco Indians, as also the missionary work done for them.

GRUBB, W. BARBROOKE. An Unknown People in an Unknown Land. pp. 330. 1911. Seeley. 16s.

A vivid account including some thrilling episodes of missionary work among the Indians of Paraguay.

GUINNESS, GERALDINE. Peru: Its Story, People, and Religion. pp. 438. 1909. Revell. $2.50.

Very attractive description of the people of Peru and their religions, with an outline of their history; reveals the condition of desperate need and scant supply.

JOHNSTON, JULIA H. Indian and Spanish Neighbors. pp 194. 1905. Revell. 35 cents, 50 cents.

Text-book for women's classes for inter-denominational use, excellent.

KEANE, A. H Central and South America. Vol. I. pp. 611. 1909. Lippincott. $5 50.

Volume I deals with the ten republics of South America, and in the main is geographical and ethnographical. Professor Keane is one of the best authorities on the subject.

MOSES, BERNARD. South America on the Eve of Emancipation. pp. 356. 1908. Putnam. $1.50.

Presents reliably some phases of Spanish colonial history and social organization which help to an understanding of modern conditions in South America.

NEELY, THOMAS B South America: Its Missionary Problems pp. 312 1909. Missionary Education Movement. 35 cents, 50 cents.

A mission study text-book on South America; not very thorough, but gives a faithful sketch of the neglected continent as a mission field.

RUHL, ARTHUR. The Other Americans. pp. 321. 1908. Scribner. $1.50.

South American cities, countries and places described in interesting chapters, which had previously appeared as articles in *Collier's* and *Scribner's Magazine*, written by a trained observer of affairs, with a sense of humor and an original style.

SCOTT-ELLIOTT, G. F. Chile. pp. 341 1910. Scribner. $3.00.

Gives an exhaustive and interesting account of the checkered history, present conditions and prospects of the country. Like the other books in *Scribner's* South American Series, it has little or nothing to say regarding religious conditions, but gives the setting without which the religious needs of the country cannot be understood.

SPEER, ROBERT E. South American Problems. pp 256. 1912. S V. M. 50 cents, 75 cents.

An account of the present conditions, economic, educational, moral and religious, in South America, a straightforward, scholarly and constructive treatment of things as they are: the outcome of much study and a personal tour of investigation; written as a text-book for student classes.

TUCKER, HUGH C. The Bible in Brazil. pp. 293. 1902. Revell. $1 25.

Though written by a Bible Society representative, the scope of the book is not limited to the work of that organization; includes the story of extensive journeys in the various States of Brazil, giving glimpses of social and religious life and of mission work.

WINTON, GEORGE BEVERLY. A New Era in Old Mexico. pp. 203 1905. Publishing House Methodist Episcopal Church South. $1.00.

Gives a sketch of Mexican history, ancient and modern, the political situation, missionary conditions and outlook; written by a former missionary there.

YOUNG, ROBERT. From Cape Horn to Panama. pp. 202. 1900. South American Missionary Society. $1.00.

Narrative of missionary enterprises among the neglected races of South America. While in the interests of a single society, it is the best picture of work among the Indians of the Southern Hemisphere.

OCEANIA

ALEXANDER, JAMES M. The Islands of the Pacific. pp. 515. 1909. American Tract Society. $2.00.

Sketch of the people and missions of various South Sea groups, with emphasis upon the transformations wrought by Christianity.

BLISS, MRS. THEODORA CROSBY. Micronesia. pp. 167. 1906. American Board. 30 cents, 50 cents.

Reveals the romance of missions in the Island world; concerned chiefly with an account of the work of the American Board, but illustrates graphically all mission work in the Pacific Islands; written from first-hand information.

BRAIN, BELLE M. The Transformation of Hawaii. pp. 193. 1898. Revell. $1 00.

Story, briefly told for young people, of the change from heathenism to incipient statehood, wrought mainly by missions of the American Board

BROOKS, ELIZABETH H. Java and its Challenge. pp. 196. 1911. Privately published. 50 cents. Copies may be ordered from Miss Elizabeth H. Brooks, Beaver, Pa.

A story of the peoples, religions and government of this interesting island, and of the missionary work now being carried on there, written primarily as a text-book for young people.

BROWN, ARTHUR J. The New Era in the Philippines. pp. 314. 1903. Revell. Out of print.

Studies of the islands made on the ground by a missionary secretary of keen discernment, although now somewhat out of date, excellent from various points of view; used as a study class text-book.

BROWN, GEORGE. George Brown, D D. An Autobiography. pp. 535. 1909. Hodder & Stoughton $3.50.

Recounts experiences of an explorer and missionary in Samoa, New Britain, New Ireland, New Guinea, and the Solomon Islands.

CENSUS OF THE PHILIPPINE ISLANDS. Vol. I. pp. 619 1905.

Contains information, the authority of which is beyond appeal, regarding the general conditions in the Philippines.

DEVINS, JOHN BANCROFT. An Observer in the Philippines. pp. 416. 1905 American Tract Society. $2 00.

A well-known editor's racy account of a trip of constant interrogation and observation in the islands; records of America's achievements and her problems, as well as those of Protestant missions.

GOMES, EDWIN H. Seventeen Years Among the Sea Dyaks of Borneo. pp. 331. 1911. Seeley. 16s

A graphic portrayal of social, moral and religious conditions among these animistic tribes in Borneo and of the triumphs of the Gospel among them, written by a pioneer missionary.

KING, JOSEPH. W. G. Lawes of Savage Island. pp. 388. 1909. Religious Tract Society. 5s.

An account of a pioneer missionary, showing what a quiet, unassuming Christian is able to accomplish among savages by his wise counsels, progressive policy and Christian life; gives the history of the establishment of missions in New Guinea; contains some valuable suggestions on the effect of government protection and on industrial work.

LAMB, ROBERT. Saints and Savages. pp. 313. 1905. W. Blackwood. 6s.

A chatty, vivid picture of life before and after Christian enlightenment, dealing mainly with natives; pathetic fiction which compels interest.

LOVETT, RICHARD. James Chalmers: His Autobiography and Letters. pp. 511. Revell. $1.50.

Standard life of one of the most famous and fearless of missionaries to South Sea cannibals, by whose hands he was murdered in 1901.

LYMAN, HENRY M. Hawaiian Yesterdays pp. 281 1906. McClurg. $2.00.

A romantic portrayal, in "Chapters from a Boy's Life in the Islands in the Early Days," of conditions in Hawaii in the first half of the last century.

MONTGOMERY, MRS. HELEN BARRETT. Christus Redemptor. pp. 282. 1906. Macmillan. 50 cents

A study of the Islands of the Pacific, including the Philippines; gives an account of the missionary work now being carried on among their inhabitants; very informing.

PATON, JAMES, editor. John G. Paton. An Autobiography. pp. 854. 1907. Revell. $1.50

Life of one of the most simple, saintly, and brave of modern missionaries; a most impressive volume

PATON, MRS. JOHN G. Letters and Sketches from the New Hebrides. pp. 382 1905. Doran. $1.75.

A supplementary volume to the life of her husband, John G. Paton; letters and sketches descriptive of missionary experiences in the South Seas, written in a charming style.

PIERSON, DELAVAN L., editor The Pacific Islanders. pp. 354. 1906. Funk & Wagnalls. $1.00.

Chapters from the life stories of famous missionaries, illustrating the Gospel's power to transform savages into saints, by various authors

STUNTZ, HOMER C. The Philippines and the Far East pp. 514. 1904. Jennings & Graham. $1.75.

Based upon a large experience and complete first-hand knowledge of the land, peoples and missionary work in the islands; valuable also from the point of view of government policies.

WILLIAMS, JOHN. Missionary Enterprises in the South Sea Islands. pp. 416. 1907. Presbyterian Board of Publication. $1.25.

Narrative of the missionary labors of a great apostle of the South Sea Islands, John Williams, the martyr of Erromanga.

WRIGHT, HAMILTON M. Handbook of the Philippines pp. 429. 1909. McClurg. $1 40.

Account of the Philippines as they are to-day; a mass of information on political and industrial matters, with a chapter on missionary work; good maps and illustrations; written by an extensive traveler and careful observer.

YONGE, CHARLOTTE M. Life of John Coleridge Patteson, Missionary Bishop of the Melanesian Islands. 2 vols. pp. 370; 411. 1894. Macmillan. $3.00.

Standard life of one of Britain's finest spirits, exhibits his humility, versatility, attractiveness, scholarship, and spirituality.

UNITED STATES AND CANADA

ANDERSON, WILBERT L. The Country Town. pp. 307. 1906. Baker & Taylor. $1.00.

A scientific and optimistic examination of the complex influences which operate upon the population of the country communities.

ARCTANDER, JOHN W. The Apostle of Alaska. pp. 385. 1909. Revell. $1 50.

Biography, full of interest and inspiration, of William Duncan, of Metlakahtla, one of the noblest of missionaries; recounts new Acts of the Apostles among the pagan Indians of the frozen North.

ATLANTA UNIVERSITY PUBLICATIONS (Atlanta University Press).

The College-Bred Negro. 1900. 25 cents.

Health and Physique of the Negro American. 1906. 75 cents.

Mortality Among Negroes in Cities. 1903. 50 cents.

The Negro Church. 1904. 50 cents.

The above-named pamphlets are the most thorough and original investigations of the negro problem that have been made.

BAKER, RAY STANNARD. Following the Color Line. pp. 314. 1908. Doubleday, Page. $2 00.

An impartial and clear statement of the negro problem, written by a Northern man who has a keen eye for facts, and sees, as few men do, the tendency of events.

BEARD, AUGUSTUS FIELD. The Story of John Frederick Oberlin. pp. 196 1909. Pilgrim Press. $1.25.

A striking and prophetic illustration, taken from Northern France a century and a half ago, of the possibilities of constructive service in rural communities

BLISS, W. D. P., editor. New Encyclopedia of Social Reform. pp. 1320 1908. Funk & Wagnalls. $7.50; $14.00.

A standard work of reference on social questions; covers a very wide range; very valuable.

BLYTHE, MARION. An American Bride in Porto Rico. pp. 205. 1911. Revell. $1.00.

Chatty letters descriptive of missionary experiences in Porto Rico; suited to reading circles of younger girl students.

BRANDENBURG, BROUGHTON. Imported Americans. pp. 303. 1904. Stokes. $1.60.

Recounts the experiences of the author and his wife while studying in disguise the immigration question.

BROOKS, JOHN GRAHAM. Social Unrest. pp. 394. 1904. Macmillan 25 cents, $1.50

An interesting, popular discussion of burning social questions

BUTTERFIELD, KENYON L. Chapters in Rural Progress. pp. 251. 1908. University of Chicago Press. $1 00.

Studies in the sociological aspects of the American rural problem and presentation of the agencies that work toward its solution.

BUTTERFIELD, KENYON L. The Country Church and the Rural Problem. pp. 153. 1911. University of Chicago Press. $1.00.

Lectures giving a strong analysis of the rural problem and the relation to it of the country church.

CALKINS, RAYMOND. Substitutes for the Saloon. pp. 397. 1901 Houghton, Mifflin. $1.30

A critical examination of many proposed solutions of the drink evil.

CLARK, JOSEPH B. Leavening the Nation. pp. 362. 1903 Baker & Taylor. $1.25.

The story of American home missions by a Congregational home missionary secretary, thoughtful, not popular.

COMMONS, JOHN R. Races and Immigrants in America. pp. 242. 1908. Macmillan. $1.50.

Scholarly examination of the problems incident to the mingling of races and especially to the additions to the population made during the nineteenth century; problems of industry, labor, crime, politics, etc., discussed by a high authority.

CONNOR, RALPH. The Life of James Robertson. pp. 412. 1908. Revell. $1.50.

Biography of a rugged prophet and statesman in Canada who summoned the Church to its work on the frontier and was a leader for many years in that work.

CONNOR, RALPH. The Foreigner. pp. 384. 1909. Hodder & Stoughton. $1.50

A story of the Canadian West, indicating the serious immigration problems existing there, and the opportunities of the Church to win victories for good citizenship

CROWELL, KATHERINE R. The Call of the Waters. pp. 157. 1908. Revell. 35 cents, 50 cents.

A study of frontier mission work in America; textbook for women's church classes.

DEFOREST, R. W., and LAWRENCE VEILLER, editors. The Tenement House Problem. 2 vols. pp. 470; 516. 1903. Macmillan. $6 00

A thorough investigation of the object named in its title; written from the point of view of the expert in social uplift work; crammed with valuable facts.

DEVINE, EDWARD T. Principles of Relief. pp. 495. 1904. Macmillan. $2.00.

A reliable treatment of this subject, written by one who, as head of the Associated Charities of New York City, has had an exceptional opportunity to verify principles in their application.

DEVINE, EDWARD T. Misery and Its Causes. pp. 274. 1909. Macmillan. $1.25.

A scientific work by a real authority on the relief of poverty, especially serviceable to those who wish to familiarize themselves rapidly with social reconstruction in the city.

DEVINE, EDWARD T. The Spirit of Social Work. pp. 231. 1911. Charity Organization Society. $1 00.

A series of sane and trenchant addresses by a foremost student of social conditions, deals with important aspects of social reclamation, such as the treatment of crime, conservation of human resources, and the religious treatment of poverty

DOUGLASS, H. PAUL. Christian Reconstruction in the South. pp. 407. 1909. Pilgrim Press. $1 50

A study of the work of the American Missionary Association in the South.

DUNCAN, NORMAN. Dr. Grenfell's Parish. pp. 155. 1905. Revell. $1.00.

A series of sketches of Dr. Grenfell and his heroic work on the Labrador coast.

DUNCAN, NORMAN. Higgins, a Man's Christian. pp. 117. 1909. Harper. 25 cents, 35 cents.

Brief character sketch of a "sky pilot" in the woods of Minnesota, and a description of his heroic work.

EELLS, M. Marcus Whitman. pp. 349. 1909. Alice Harriman Co. $2.50.

Best account of the life of the great pathfinder of the Northwest.

FOWLES, G. M. Down in Porto Rico. pp. 163. 1906 Eaton & Mains. 75 cents.

A readable survey of modern conditions in the island; written from first-hand observation.

GLADDEN, WASHINGTON. Applied Christianity. pp 320. 1886. Houghton, Mifflin. $1.50.

Frank and stimulating addresses by a well-known thinker on social questions on the mission of Christianity in the solution of such problems.

GRENFELL, W. T., and OTHERS. Labrador. pp. 497. 1909. Macmillan. $2.25.

Best description of this unfamiliar land and its people.

GRENFELL, W. T. The Harvest of the Sea. pp. 162 1905. Revell. $1.00.

Vivid account of the life of the North Sea fishermen and of Christianity working among them, a romance of missions.

GROSE, HOWARD B. Aliens or Americans. pp. 337. 1906. Missionary Education Movement. 35 cents, 50 cents.

Best text-book for study classes on the immigration problem.

GROSE, HOWARD B. Advance in the Antilles. pp 259. 1910. Missionary Education Movement. 35 cents, 50 cents.

A readable and reliable account of present-day conditions in Cuba and Porto Rico, with special reference to the missionary work and outlook in these islands; written as a text-book for young people.

HADLEY, S. H. Down in Water Street pp. 242 1902. Revell. $1.00.

A largely autobiographical sketch of work in the famous rescue mission founded by Jerry McAuley.

HALL, PRESCOTT F. Immigration pp. 393 1906 Holt. $1 50.

A standard work on immigration; treats of the history, causes and conditions of immigration and its effect upon the United States, includes the history of past legislation upon the subject, one section devoted to Chinese immigration.

HART, A. B. The Southern South. pp. 445. 1910. Appleton. $1.50.

An examination of present conditions and problems in the South, bringing into relief those of its characteristics which are not shared by the North.

HELM, MARY. The Upward Path pp 333. 1909. Missionary Education Movement. 35 cents, 50 cents.

A discriminating study of the negro problem and the uplifting power of Christ as its chief solution, written as a text-book for young people's classes.

HENDERSON, CHARLES R, editor. Modern Methods of Charity. pp. 715. 1904. Macmillan. $3.50

Covers satisfactorily the field of public relief throughout the world, the chapters on the different countries being written by experts, contains an interesting section on the Jews and their charitable organizations.

HENDERSON, CHARLES R. Social Settlements. pp 196. 1907. Wessels 60 cents.

Description of social movements in the United States, with a catalogue of the chief settlements now in existence.

HENDERSON, CHARLES R. Social Duties From the Christian Point of View. pp. 332 1909 University of Chicago Press. $1 25.

A suggestive, interesting, and very valuable book on social problems, specially arranged for class-room studies; written by one who has had wide experience in these matters.

HODGES, GEORGE. Faith and Social Service. pp. 270 1906. Whittaker. $1.25.

Eight lectures delivered by Dean Hodges before the Lowell Institute on the main elements in the social problem.

HOFFMAN, FREDERICK L. Race Traits and Tendencies of the American Negro pp 329. 1896 American Economic Association. $1.25, $2.00.

The most exhaustive single study of population, birth and death rates, anthropometry, etc., of the negro race in America.

HUNTER, ROBERT. Poverty pp. 382. 1905. Macmillan. 25 cents, $2.00.

Gives the main facts concerning the nature and extent of poverty in the United States and a clear idea of the tremendous draft which that country is drawing on the future in allowing a condition of inadequate relief and half-hearted constructive work to remain

JOHNSTON, JULIA H. Indian and Spanish Neighbors. pp. 194. 1905 Revell. 35 cents, 50 cents.

A text-book covering briefly the needs and opportunities for work among the Indians and Spanish-speaking people in the United States and in Cuba and Porto Rico

KILDARE, OWEN. My Old Bailiwick pp. 313. 1906. Revell $1.50.

Vivid pictures of tragedy and sin in the Lower East Side of New York City, by a well-known novelist who had lived there, depressing, but true; gives the summons of awful need.

LEUPP, FRANCIS E. The Indian and His Problem. pp. 369. 1910. Scribner. $1.50

An impartial discussion of the American Indians by one who has studied their character, history and relation to the United States Government, valuable in the study of the problem of evangelizing the Red Man.

MCLANAHAN, SAMUEL. Our People of Foreign Speech. pp. 111. 1904 Revell. 50 cents.

A handbook distinguishing and describing those in the United States whose native tongue is other than English.

MATHEWS, SHAILER. The Church and the Changing Order. pp. 255. 1909. Macmillan. $1 50.

A study of the rightful place of the Church in the solution of the desperate social problems of our day

MATHEWS, SHAILER. The Social Teachings of Jesus. pp. 235. 1909. University of Chicago Press 50 cents.

An effort to discover the mind of the Master concerning the great social problems of our day, by a well-known writer on social questions.

MILLER, K. Race Adjustment. pp. 306. 1908 Neale. $2 00.

A clear, strong statement from a scholarly negro professor, dealing with social, educational, and religious problems of the Negro race; most of the chapters written from the standpoint of a social student and therefore without bias; others show a touch of race antagonism.

MUIR, WILLIAM. Christianity and Labor. pp. 316. 1911. Hodder & Stoughton. $1.50

A careful and optimistic study of the labor question, made by a well-known Scottish minister; traces the laborer's progress through his condition as slave, serf, servant and employee towards the Christian ideal, which the last chapter describes.

MURPHY, EDGAR G. The Present South. pp. 288. 1904. Longmans. $1 50.

A book largely devoted to the negro problem in the South, written by a scholarly Southern man, deals largely with the educational problem, and is perhaps the best plea for negro education now published.

MURPHY, EDGAR G The Basis of Ascendancy. pp 248. 1909. Longmans. $1.50.

An "explicit statement of those fundamental principles of policy" which underlie the solution of the race question; absolutely fair and Christian in spirit.

NEW YORK CHARITIES DIRECTORY. pp. 835. 1911. Charity Organization Society. $1.00

Valuable for reference in a study of the social problems of the city; reveals the scope and variety of the work of organized charity to-day.

PAGE, THOMAS NELSON. The Negro, the Southerner's Problem. pp. 324. 1904. Scribner. $1.25.

Characterized by thorough familiarity with the "old-time" negro, with less accurate knowledge of present conditions; prone to magnify all the virtues of the slave and all the vices of the present negro.

PEABODY, F. G. Jesus Christ and the Social Question pp. 374. 1900. Macmillan. $1 50.

A scholarly and suggestive appeal from the spirit and teaching of Jesus in regard to the social issues of the hour.

PEABODY, F. G. The Approach to the Social Question. pp. 210. 1909. Macmillan. $1.25.

An introduction to the study of the social sciences; useful to those who are expecting to undertake any form of social work.

PEILE, JAMES H. F. The Reproach of the Gospel. pp 199. 1907. Longmans $1.80

Bampton lectures for 1907; an unexaggerated statement of the social evils existing in Christian countries and a call to the Church to reckon these evils as her problem.

PHILLIPS, A. L. The Call of the Home Land. pp. 173. 1906. Presbyterian Committee of Publication. 40 cents.

A sketch in broad outline of the many problems classed under the general head of home missions; has been widely used as a text-book for study classes.

PLATT, WARD. The Frontier. pp. 292. 1908. Missionary Education Movement. 35 cents, 50 cents.

A text-book for study classes of young people, dealing with home missionary opportunities on the new American frontier.

RAUSCHENBUSCH, W. Christianity and the Social Crisis. pp. 429. 1907. Macmillan. $1.50.

An admirable treatise on the social mission of Christianity and the stake of the Church in the social movements of to-day.

RICHMOND, MARY E. The Good Neighbor. pp. 152. 1908. Lippincott. 60 cents.

Simple guide to an understanding of organized charity; full of practical suggestions.

ROBERTS, PETER. Immigrant Races in America. pp. 109. 1910. Association Press. 50 cents.

Gives in brief the main lines of American immigration; written by one of America's leading authorities on this subject.

RUSSELL, CHARLES E. B and RIGBY, LILLIAN M. Working Lads' Clubs. pp. 445. 1908. Macmillan. $1.50.

A description of the working of these clubs in Great Britain and their part in solving the problem of the working boy; with a list of the clubs in operation in the British Isles.

RIIS, JACOB A. How the Other Half Lives pp. 304. 1890. Scribner. $1.25.

Presents facts that every one in "comfortable circumstances" ought to know, paints a sad picture, but not without its bright lights of unconquerable souls; written by a well-known and sympathetic student of social questions.

SHELTON, DON O. Heroes of the Cross in America. pp. 298. 1904. Missionary Education Movement. 50 cents.

Brief sketches of the lives of men who in Christ's name have labored for the uplifting of society in America; written for young people's classes.

SHERWOOD, JAMES M. Memoirs of David Brainerd. pp 354 1884 Funk & Wagnalls $1 50.

Standard life of the great apostle to the American Indians.

SOCIAL EVIL, THE. pp 188. 1902. Putnam. Out of print.

A report prepared under direction of the Committee of Fifteen.

SPARGO, JOHN. Socialism. pp 349. 1906. Macmillan $1.25.

A clear and enthusiastic presentation of Socialism; immensely interesting and useful, in spite of the writer's occasional tendency toward exaggeration.

STEFFENS, LINCOLN The Shame of the Cities. pp. 310. 1904. McClure $1.20

An unsparing exposure of corruption in high places as well as low in some of the leading cities of the United States.

STEINER, EDWARD A. Against the Current. pp. 230. 1910 Revell. $1.25.

Interesting chapters of autobiography; throws much light on the immigrant problem

STEINER, EDWARD A On the Trail of the Immigrant. pp. 375. 1906. Revell. $1 50

An interesting study of race characteristics written out of intimate experience and ripe scholarship; considers the immigrant in both his old home and his new.

STEINER, EDWARD A. The Immigrant Tide. pp. 370 1909. Revell. $1.50.

An equally keen and reliable volume, in which Professor Steiner studies the immigrant wave in its flow and ebb between America and Europe These two volumes are invaluable to anyone studying this great problem

STELZLE, CHARLES. The Working Man and Social Problems. pp. 166 1903. Revell 75 cents.

Reveals the life and heart of the working man and offers suggestions as to how the Church may help him, written by one who by experience knows the feelings and aspirations of working men.

STELZLE, CHARLES. Christianity's Storm Centre. pp. 240. 1907. Revell. $1 00.

Another volume on the Church and the laboring classes by the official representative to labor of one of the leading church communions; dwells on the Church's opportunity to avert grave dangers and win great victories among the working classes.

STEPHENSON, G. T. Race Distinctions in American Law. pp 338. 1910. Appleton. $1.50.

Study of the laws of the states and of the nation in their bearing on the negro question; examines the limitations either allowed or imposed by law upon the negro.

STEWART, ROBERT L. Sheldon Jackson. pp. 488. 1908. Revell. $2.00.

Best life of the well-known pioneer missionary to Alaska.

STRONG, JOSIAH. The Challenge of the City. pp. 327. 1907. Missionary Education Movement. 35 cents, 50 cents.

Excellent text-book for study classes on the present-day problems of the city, from the pen of an authority.

STRONG, JOSIAH. Social Progress. pp. 275. 1906. Baker & Taylor. $1.00.

A compilation of statistics of agencies engaged in welfare work.

THE SURVEY (March, '11—Sept., '11). pp. 897. The Charity Organization. $2.00.

Latest volume of the official organ of the Charity Organization Society of New York; best general periodical on social questions.

TUTTLE, DAVID SYLVESTER. Reminiscences of a Missionary Bishop. pp. 489. 1906. Whittaker. $2.00.

Autobiographical records of the work of a heroic and statesmanlike missionary bishop in Montana, Idaho, and Utah; graphic description of frontier work; contains a careful examination of the Mormon system.

WARNER, AMOS G. American Charities. pp. 510. 1908. Crowell. $2.00.

The first attempt to cover systematically the field of American charities and to formulate the principles of relief which had been evolved from a century of benevolence; brought down to date in the second edition.

WASHINGTON, BOOKER T. Up From Slavery. pp. 330. 1907. Burt. 50 cents.

An inspiring biography of an inspiring life, giving the story of one who lives above the prejudice of race, and is doing a marvelous work for his people.

WASHINGTON, BOOKER T. The Story of the Negro. 2 vols. pp. 332; 437. 1909. Doubleday, Page. $1.50.

A record of what the negro himself has accomplished in elevating himself to a higher civilization; does not deal with what is known as the negro problem. In the first volume the negro is seen in Africa and as a slave; in the second the negro as a free man is discussed.

WASHINGTON, BOOKER T. Working with the Hands. pp. 250. 1904. Doubleday, Page. $1.50.

A splendid story of the Tuskegee Institute and a powerful argument for industrial education.

WASHINGTON, BOOKER T., and DUBOIS, W. E. D. The Negro in the South. 1907. Jacobs. $1.00.

Deals with the economic and religious life of the negro.

WEATHERFORD, W. D. Negro Life in the South. pp. 183. 1910. Association Press. 50 cents.

By all means the best text-book for student classes on the negro question; suitable also for general reading; a safe and sane treatment of a difficult and delicate question, showing both scholarship and Christian spirit

WELLS, MRS. D. B., and OTHERS. The Conservation of National Ideals. pp. 187. 1911. Revell. 35 cents, 50 cents.

A sketchy, popular survey of some of the acute home problems confronting the Christians of America and a summons to effort for their solution; written for women's Church classes; should be useful for classes composed of younger students.

WELLS, HERBERT G. New Worlds for Old. pp. 333. 1909. Macmillan. $1.50.

Vivid presentation of his socialistic faith by this wide-awake writer of queer romances.

WILSON, WARREN H. The Church of the Open Country. pp. 238. 1911. Missionary Education Movement. 35 cents, 50 cents.

One of America's foremost students of the rural problem here sets forth the conditions and necessities of country communities and indicates the opportunity and office of the Church in meeting a pressing situation; a thoughtful study of the question, prepared for use in mission study classes.

WOOD, H. G. Personal Economy and Social Reform. pp. 146. 1912. Association Press. 50 cents.

An interesting examination of the problems involved in the earning and spending of money; deals with the question from a humanitarian point of view and then points out clearly the Christian implications of the problem.

WOOD, ROBERT. Americans in Process. pp. 389. 1900. Houghton, Mifflin. $1.50.

One phase of the immigration problem; a study of the change of population incident to new arrivals in South End, Boston.

YOUNG, EGERTON R. By Canoe and Dog Train. pp. 267. 1899. Revell. $1.25.

In many respects the best volume by the well-known ex-missionary to the Indians of British America, full of stirring scenes of life and work among these people.

UNOCCUPIED FIELDS

BUDGE, E. A. T. The Egyptian Sudan: Its History and Monuments. 2 vols pp. 652; 618. 1909. Lippincott. $3.00.

Two elaborate volumes on the history of exploration, the antiquities and archæological discoveries of the Egyptian Sudan, showing the early civilization, the effect of the Mohammedan invasion, and the awful rule of the Mahdi, with a sketch of the present missionary enterprise, and an elaborate bibliography of the Sudan.

BISHOP, ISABELLA B. Among the Tibetans. pp. 159. 1894. Revell. $1.50.

Interesting sketch of the first journey of this intrepid explorer; information no longer up to date.

COBBALD, RALPH P. Innermost Asia. 1900. Scribner. $5.00.

A further contribution to the problem of the exploration of Central Asia, supplements earlier books and is specially full on the desert stretches west of China.

CAREY, WILLIAM T. Adventures in Tibet. pp. 285. 1901. United Society of Christian Endeavor. $1.50.

A bright, readable book, which gives a picture of the land as a whole, and also the original diary of the astonishing journey of Miss Taylor in 1892-1893; written by a well-known missionary in India.

DE LESDAIN, COUNT. From Pekin to Sikkim. pp. 301. 1908. Dutton. $1.50.

An account of a remarkable journey, a wedding tour, which touches on many regions which are unknown or scarcely known to Westerners, very interesting.

DAVIS, RICHARD HARDING. The Congo and the Coasts of Africa. pp. 220. 1909. Scribner. $1.50.

A traveler's indictment of Belgian rule on the Congo, with a chapter on the work of American traders, but none on that of American missionaries.

DENNETT, R. E. At the Back of the Black Man's Mind. (Somaliland.) pp. 288. 1909. Macmillan. $1.50.

A book on comparative religion intended to show that concurrent with fetichism there is a higher conception of God in the African mind; emphasizes the importance of the kingly office among the pagan tribes of Western Africa.

DOUGHTY, CHARLES M. Wanderings in Arabia. 2 vols. pp. 309; 297 1908. Scribner. $4.50.

A reprint of his "Arabia Deserta," describing three years' explorations in the heart of Arabia; interesting in style, written by a prince among explorers.

FIELD, CLAUD. With the Afghans. pp. 221. 1908. Marshall Bros. 3s. 6d.

A story of the Afghan problem by a missionary at Peshawar, proving that the Gospel goes where the missionary cannot, and that the great closed land has already yielded converts and martyrs

FRASER, DAVID. The Marches of Hindustan. pp. 521. 1907. Blackwood. 21s.

A popular account of the regions bordering India, including Tibet and Afghanistan; valuable for its maps and tables.

GUINNESS, GERALDINE. Peru: Its Story, People, and Religion pp. 438. 1909. Revell $1 50.

A fascinating study of one of the most interesting countries of South America; a plea for the occupation of this field.

HAMILTON, ANGUS Afghanistan pp. 562. 1906. Scribner. $5.00

An exhaustive treatise on this unoccupied field; especially full of geographical and political information, with a careful study of the people and the absolute rule under which they live.

HEDIN, SVEN Through Asia 2 vols. pp. 649; 606. 1898. Harper. $10 00

Two magnificent volumes by this prince of explorers, with nearly 300 illustrations and photographs describing his journeys through Central Asia from 1893 to 1897.

HERBERT, AGNES Two Dianas in Somaliland. pp. 306. 1908. Lane. $4.00.

The record of a shooting trip of two English women in British Somaliland; gives an interesting glimpse of the country, and tells something of its people

HOGARTH, DAVID G. The Penetration of Arabia. pp. 359. 1904. Stokes. $1.35

A study of all the literature of Arabian travel by one who, although not himself an explorer, is thoroughly acquainted with the subject; valuable maps and illustrations of this great unknown land.

HUNTINGTON, ELLSWORTH. The Pulse of Asia. pp. 415. 1907. Houghton, Mifflin. $3.50.

Results of a scientific expedition into the heart of Asia by an American geographer; illustrates the relation between physical environment and civilization in the plateau and deserts from the Vale of Kashmir to Chinese Turkestan.

KUMM, H. KARL W. The Sudan pp. 224. 1906 Marshall Bros. 3s. 6d.

A series of chapters somewhat carelessly put together and not remarkable for style, but strong in their appeal and in the presentation of facts; the only book from a missionary standpoint on this field.

LANDON, PERCIVAL. The Opening of Tibet. pp 484. 1905 Doubleday, Page $3.80

An account of Lhasa and Central Tibet in connection with the mission sent by the British Government in 1903-4, written by the special correspondent of *The London Times*, accompanying this mission; valuable illustrations and maps.

LEES, G. ROBINSON The Witness of the Wilderness. pp. 222 1909. Longmans. $1 25.

A study of Bedouin home life, social customs and superstitions, together with an account of the new railway in Northern Arabia.

LEONARD, A. G The Lower Niger and Its Tribes. pp 564 1909 Macmillan. $1 50

A sociological study of the tribes on the Lower Niger by a British officer deeply interested in comparative religion; gives the philosophy of the people, expressed in words, proverbs and fables; their natural religion, spirit worship, and demonology are carefully treated.

MACKAY, KENNETH. Across Papua. pp. 192. 1909. Scribner. $2.50.

An account of the voyage of a scientific commission around, and their march across, the practically unknown land of Papua. The commission was appointed to inquire into the present condition of British New Guinea and the best means for its improvement.

MARTIN, FRANK A. Under the Absolute Amir pp. 330. 1907. Harper. $2.25

The observations and experiences of one who was for eight years an engineer and the only Englishman in Kabul; a picture of Islam in its awful, when untrammeled, political, social and moral results.

PENNELL, T. L. Among the Wild Tribes of the Afghan Frontier. pp 324. 1909 Lippincott. $3 50.

Fascinating description of a pioneer medical missionary's work on the border of Afghanistan; contains an account of the customs and traditions of the Afghans.

RIJNHART, SUSIE C With the Tibetans in Tent and Temple. pp. 397. 1901. Revell. $1.50.

Story of four years' residence on the Tibetan border and a journey into the interior, where Dr. Rijnhart lost her husband and baby; thrilling in some sections.

TATE, G. P The Frontiers of Baluchistan. pp. 260. 1909. Scribner. $5 00

Sketches of the desert and desert life on the borders of Persia and Afghanistan by an Indian surveyor who loves the desert and has been a wanderer all his days.

YOUNGHUSBAND, F. E The Heart of a Continent. (Central Asia.) pp. 332. 1896. Scribner. $2.00.

A narrative of travels during ten years in Manchuria, across the Gobi Desert, through the Himalayas, the Pamirs and Hunza, written by the British Commissioner for Tibet Frontier matters

ZWEMER, SAMUEL M. The Unoccupied Mission Fields of Africa and Asia. pp. 258. 1911. S. V. M. 50 cents, $1.00.

A more thorough treatment of this subject than can be found in any other volume; footnotes and an excellent bibliography open the way for more exhaustive study; partly the product of investigations made by Commission I of the World Missionary Conference; a text-book for mission study classes.

JEWS

BARON, DAVID. A Divine Forecast of Jewish History. pp. 90. Morgan & Scott. London 1s.

Gives an account of Jewish history, especially as the fulfillment of prophecy, and a forecast, according to Scripture, of the future of the nation, written by a devout and thoughtful convert from Judaism.

GIDNEY, W. T. The Jews and Their Evangelization. pp. 128 1907. Student Volunteer Missionary Union. $1 25.

Study class text-book written by a specialist, giving salient facts concerning the Jews of every period, as well as an account of missions among them.

STARCH, HERM L. Year Book of the Evangelical Missions among the Jews. 1906 Heinrichs'sche Buchhandlung. 65 cents.

Historical sketch of the International Missionary Conference, with papers in English and German read at the meeting in Amsterdam; appended is a statistical review of Jewish missions by the Rev. Louis Meyer.

THOMPSON, A. E. A Century of Jewish Missions. pp. 286. 1902. Revell. $1.00.

Though marred by many misstatements, this is a readable and generally satisfactory brief volume on the subject.

WILKINSON, SAMUEL H. In the Land of the North. pp. 105. 1905. Marshall Bros 3s. 6d.

Description of conditions and work among the Jews of Russia, from Scriptural, political, and missionary standpoints, much valuable information; by an authority on Jewish missions.

WILKINSON, SAMUEL H. The Life of John Wilkinson. pp. 350. 1908. Morgan & Scott. 1s

Life of a celebrated missionary to the Jews and a founder of the Mildmay Mission; written by his son.

STORIES AND BOOKS FOR READING CIRCLES

BAIRD, ANNIE L. A. Daybreak in Korea. pp. 123. 1909. Revell. 60 cents.

Story of a Korean girl's childhood and unhappy marriage, and of the transformation of her home by the Gospel's influence.

BALDWIN, OLIVIA A. Sita. pp. 353 1911. Revell. $1 25.

A story revealing the bondage of child marriage in India and typifying the sorrows and struggles of Indian womanhood; written by a medical missionary.

BRAIN, BELLE M. The Transformation of Hawaii. pp. 193. 1898. Revell. $1.00.

An account of one of the miracles of missions.

BRAIN, BELLE M. Fifty Missionary Stories. pp. 225. 1902 Revell. 60 cents.

BRAIN, BELLE M. Missionary Readings. pp. 235. Revell. 60 cents.

Two volumes of short sketches covering a wide variety of missionary themes and countries.

BROOMHALL, MARSHALL Dr. Lee. pp. 61. 1908. China Inland Mission 6d.

A brief authoritative narrative of a young Chinese Christian of ability and rare spiritual power; illustrates the power of the Gospel and the value of educational missions.

BUNKER, ALONZO. Sketches from the Karen Hills. pp 215. 1910. Revell. $1.00.

Vivid descriptions of native and missionary life in Burma; written in an entertaining style; suitable for reading circles.

CARMICHAEL, AMY WILSON-. Things As They Are pp. 303. 1906. Revell. $1.00.

CARMICHAEL, AMY WILSON-. Overweights of Joy. pp. 300. 1906. Revell. $1.00.

Attractively written descriptions of work among women and girls in Southern India by a cultured and devoted missionary; the first volume revealing the awful power of caste, and the second illustrating the superior power of the Gospel.

CHAMBERLAIN, JACOB. The Cobra's Den. pp. 270. 1900. Revell. $1.00.

CHAMBERLAIN, JACOB. In the Tiger Jungle. pp. 218. Revell. $1.00.

Two books of stories vividly portraying missionary work in India; by a famous veteran, recently deceased.

CONNOR, RALPH. The Foreigner. pp. 384. 1909. Hodder & Stoughton. $1.50.

CONNOR, RALPH. The Prospector. pp. 401. 1904. Revell. $1.50.

CONNOR, RALPH. Black Rock pp. 322. 1900. Revell. $1.50.

Well-known tales revealing the problems of mission work in the Canadian Northwest and the responsiveness of rough and hardened men to the uncompromising, manly presentation of the Gospel.

DE GRUCHÉ, KINGSTON. Dr. Apricot of Heaven Below. pp. 143. 1911. Revell. $1.00.

A graphic description of present-day medical work in China; by a missionary of the Church Missionary Society, at Hangchow.

DELOREY, EUSTACHE and D. SLADEN. Queer Things About Persia. pp. 381. 1907. Lippincott. $3.50.

A miniature museum of things bizarre, as noted by these well-known observers in the Empire of the Shah.

DUNCAN, NORMAN. Dr. Grenfell's Parish. pp. 155. 1905 Revell $1.00

A novelist's vivid, though brief, portrayal of the personality and self-denying labors of the famous physician to deep-sea fishermen and the Eskimos of the Labrador Coast.

DUNCAN, NORMAN. Higgins, A Man's Christian. pp. 117. 1909 Harper 25 cents, 35 cents.

A short narrative, by a well-known novelist, of a home missionary, winning men in the woods of Minnesota.

DYE, MRS. R. J. Bolenge pp. 225. 1909. Foreign Christian Missionary Society. 50 cents

Sketches descriptive of missionary life and work on the Congo.

DYER, HELEN S. Pandita Ramabai. pp. 197. Revised 1911. Revell. $1.25.

Interesting life of a talented Indian woman and an account of her work for widows of India.

ELMORE, MAUD JOHNSON. The Revolt of Sundaramma. pp. 160. 1911. Revell. $1 00.

An unusual missionary tale, only too true to life, describing the life of a real Hindu girl and her revolt against child marriage; a most attractively written story, made doubly instructive by the notes in the appendix, descriptive of Hindu life, customs and beliefs.

FAHS, MRS. SOPHIA M. Uganda's White Man of Work. pp. 289. 1907. Missionary Education Movement. 35 cents, 50 cents.

Story of the life and work of Mackay, of Uganda, told for young people.

FENN, COURTENAY H. Over Against the Treasury pp. 100. 1910 The Westminster Press 10 cents, 60 cents.,

A fine piece of missionary fiction, exposing the cheapness and selfishness of much of the criticism of missions.

GALE, JAMES S The Vanguard. pp. 320. 1904. Revell $1.50.

A novel of missionary work in Korea by a missionary of experience and insight and literary skill.

GALE, JAMES S. Korean Sketches. pp. 256. 1898. Revell. $1 00.

Portrays graphically the people of Korea and their daily life, of more than usual interest.

GRENFELL, WILFRED T. Adrift on an Ice Pan. pp 69. 1909. Houghton, Mifflin. 75 cents.

Short story of one of Dr. Grenfell's many thrilling experiences; reveals the heroism, resourcefulness and faith of the man.

GRIFFIS, WILLIAM E. Japan in History, Folk-Lore and Art. pp. 244 1906. Houghton, Mifflin 75 cents

Occupied mainly with the political history of Japan, but contains also interesting information about the customs and folklore of the people.

GRIFFIS, WILLIAM E. The Unmannerly Tiger. pp. 155. 1911. Crowell. $1.00.

A charming collection of folk stories of the Koreans, giving a peep into the Korean mind; interesting to children, both young and otherwise.

GRIFFITH, MRS. M. E. HUME-. Behind the Veil in Persia and Turkish Arabia. pp. 336. 1909. Lippincott. $3.50.

A true and vivid picture of the social and domestic life of Mohammedan women; written by one who has lived among them for eight years as the wife of a medical missionary, reveals the influence of Islam upon girlhood and womanhood.

GRIGGS, WILLIAM CHARLES. Odds and Ends from Pagoda Land. pp. 277. 1906. American Baptist Publication Society. 90 cents.

Picturesque glimpses of the life of the Burmans and Shans; seen through the eyes of a medical missionary.

GUERNSEY, ALICE M. Citizens of To-morrow. pp 160. 1907. Revell 50 cents

Short studies of many of the foreign elements in the American population; abounds in quotations; prepared for text-book use among the women of the churches.

GUTHAPFEL, MINERVA L. The Happiest Girl in Korea pp. 106. 1911. Revell. 60 cents

Bright sketches of life, chiefly child life, in the Land of Morning Calm; written either as true stories or closely founded on facts, by a missionary who evidently loves and knows the Koreans.

HARBAND, BEATRICE M. The Pen of Brahma. pp 320 1905. Revell $1.25.

Accurately described by the sub-title, "Peeps Into Hindu Hearts and Homes"; written by an experienced missionary in Southern India.

HATTERSLEY, CHARLES W Uganda by Pen and Camera. pp. 138. 1907. American Sunday School Union. $1 00.

Another good book for reading circles, entertaining sketches, full of information regarding one of the great mission fields of Africa.

HESTON, WINIFRED. A Blue Stocking in India pp. 226. 1910. Revell. $1.00.

Cleverly written letters of a lady doctor in the Marathi country, accurate in their portrayal of missionary life in that part of India, admirable for reading circles.

HUBBARD, ETHEL D. Under Marching Orders. pp. 211. 1909. Missionary Education Movement. 35 cents, 50 cents.

Life story of Mrs. Mary Porter Gamewell, of China, includes thrilling experiences during the siege of Peking

JOHNSTON, HOWARD A. The Famine and the Bread. pp. 164. 1908. Association Press. $1.00.

A good introduction to elementary general knowledge of missions; typical anecdotes of seven great fields, gathered on the ground; many illustrations

LAMBERT, JOHN C. The Romance of Missionary Heroism pp. 346. 1907. Lippincott. $1.50.

Narratives illustrating the devotion and heroism of missionaries, romantic and authentic; excellent for reading circles of younger students.

LEE, ADA, MRS. An Indian Priestess: the Life of Chundra Lela. pp. 121. 1902. Morgan & Scott. 1s. 10d.

The remarkable life story of a Hindu priestess and her work as a Christian evangelist.

LITTLE, F. The Lady of the Decoration. pp. 231. 1906. Century Company. $1.00.

A bright little story located in Japan, furnishes an attractive introduction of the uninformed and uninterested to the subject of missions

LOTI, PIERRE. Disenchanted pp. 380 1906. Macmillan. $1.50.

A narrative by the well-known French novelist; does not refer to missions, but frankly discloses the unfortunate conditions surrounding Mohammedan women.

MASON, CAROLINE A. The Little Green God. pp. 146. 1902 Revell. 75 cents.

A short satirical novel of wide popularity; teaches wholesome missionary lessons.

MAXWELL, ELLEN B. The Bishop's Conversion pp 384 1892. Eaton & Mains. $1.50

A book of fiction portraying real missionary life in India; likely to remove misunderstanding and prejudice

NOBLE, W. ARTHUR. Ewa, A Tale of Korea. pp 354. 1906 Eaton & Mains. $1 25

A recent book of missionary fiction dealing with Korean life and customs.

OXENHAM, JOHN White Fire. pp. 366. 1906. American Tract Society. $1.25.

A romantic tale, revealing the adventurous and self-sacrificing life of James Chalmers, good for younger students.

PIERSON, ARTHUR T. The Miracles of Missions. Four series pp. 196; 223; 265; 257. Various dates. Funk & Wagnalls. First three series, 35 cents, $1.00. Fourth series, 30 cents, 90 cents.

Four volumes full of well-selected triumphs of Christian missions in the lives of individuals and communities, has strong apologetic value both for Christianity and for missions; written by the well-known editor of the "Missionary Review of the World," recently deceased.

Quirmbach, A. P. From Opium Fiend to Preacher. pp. 181. Musson. 75 cents.

Striking tale of an actual miracle of transformation; written by a Canadian missionary to China.

Richmond, Mary E. The Good Neighbor. pp. 152. 1908. Lippincott. 60 cents.

A straightforward, practical little volume on the city problem, by the general secretary of the Philadelphia Society for Organizing Charity.

Sheets, Emily T. In Kali's Country. pp. 208. 1910 Revell. $1.00.

Stories, some of them quite imaginative, illustrating the need and progress of missionary work among the masses of India's population, show that the writer made her tour through India with eyes and ears wide open.

Springer, Helen E. Snapshots From Sunny Africa. pp. 194. 1909. Revell. $1.00.

Pen pictures of missionary life in Africa; attractively written.

Steiner, Edward A. The Mediator. pp. 356. 1907. Revell. $1 50.

A novel dealing with the immigrant problem in America; by an authority on the immigration question.

Taylor, Mrs. Howard. In the Far East pp. 178. 1907. China Inland Mission $1.25.

Letters and addresses of Mrs. Howard Taylor; very brightly written; give glimpses into Chinese hearts and homes, and the work of the China Inland Mission.

Taylor, Mrs. Howard. Pastor Hsi: Confucian Scholar and Christian. pp. 494. 1907 China Inland Mission. $1.50

Strong apologetic for missions; a startling modern miracle; combines in one the two earlier volumes describing Hsi respectively before and after his conversion.

Van Sommer, Annie, and Zwemer, S. M., editors. Our Moslem Sisters pp. 299. 1907 Revell. $1.25.

A symposium, carefully edited, on the status and treatment of women in Mohammedan countries.

✓ **Welsh, Beatrice W.** An African Girl. pp. 96. 1909 Oliphant 15 cents, 60 cents.

Descriptive of girl life from birth to marriage in Southern Nigeria; written for young people.

White, H. C The Days of June. pp. 122. 1909. Revell. 50 cents.

Story, simply and impressively told, of a Southern girl of rare winsomeness who laid down her life, at an early age, for China

Williams, Mrs. Isabella B. By the Great Wall. pp. 400. 1909. Revell. $1.50.

Selected correspondence of Mrs. Williams, revealing a life of patient, active missionary service at the Northern gateway of China.

Wilson, Samuel G. Mariam: A Romance of Persia. pp. 122. 1906. American Tract Society. 50 cents.

A story from real life, disguised as fiction, faithfully portraying conditions and missionary work among the Armenians of Persia.

Yonge, Charlotte M. The Making of a Missionary, or Day-Dreams in Earnest. pp. 228 1900. Whittaker. $1.00

Tells how an English girl realized in China her early dreams of missionary service.

Young, Egerton R. By Canoe and Dog Train. pp. 267. 1890. Eaton & Mains $1 25.

Graphic descriptions of missionary work among the Indians of the Canadian Northwest.

PASTOR'S WORKING LIBRARY ON MISSIONS

Barton, James L Daybreak in Turkey. pp 306 1908 Pilgrim Press 50 cents, $1.50.

Admirable sketch of Protestant missions in the Turkish Empire to date; fine presentation of the changed conditions there.

Barton, James L. The Missionary and His Critics. pp. 235. 1906. Revell. $1.00

Packed with quotations from eminent men as to the necessity, value, and success of Christian missions

Barton, James L. The Unfinished Task. pp. 211. 1908 S. V. M. 35 cents, 50 cents.

A lucid statement of the magnificent scope and present status of the missionary enterprise

Beach, Harlan P. Dawn on the Hills of T'ang. pp 227 1905. S. V. M. 25 cents, 50 cents.

A scholarly, severely condensed account of China as a mission field, by a leading authority

Blaikie, W. G The Personal Life of David Livingstone. pp. 508. 1880. Revell. $1.50.

The standard life of Livingstone.

Brown, Arthur J. The Foreign Missionary. pp 412 1907. S. V M 68 cents. Revell. $1.50.

Indispensable to the pastor who wishes to know the genius, workings and relationships of the foreign missionary enterprise.

Bryson, Mrs. Mary T. John Kenneth Mackenzie. pp. 404. Revell. $1.50.

Best life of the most noted medical missionary to China.

Carmichael, Amy Wilson-. Things as They Are. pp. 303. 1906 Revell. $1.00.

Sketches showing graphically the blackness of idolatry and the caste system in Southern India

Carver, William O. Missions in the Plan of the Ages pp. 289. 1909. Revell. $1 25.

Scholarly treatment of the place of missions in the revealed will of God.

Cary, Otis. Japan and Its Regeneration. pp. 159. 1908. S. V. M. 35 cents, 50 cents.

Excellent brief account of Japan and the history and opportunity of Protestant missions there; written by a leading authority.

Church and Missionary Education, The. pp. 320. 1908. Missionary Education Movement. 35 cents

Report of the Convention of the Young People's Missionary Movement, Pittsburg, 1908.

Clark, Francis E., and Harriet A. The Gospel in Latin Lands pp. 315. 1909 Macmillan 35 cents.

The mission of the Gospel to the Latin countries of Europe and America

CLARKE, WILLIAM NEWTON. A Study of Christian Missions. pp. 268 1900. Scribner. $1.25.

. One of the most thoughtful and suggestive volumes on missions and mission theory, written from the modern point of view.

CLEMENT, E. W A Handbook of Modern Japan. , pp. 423. 1905. McClurg. $1.40.

Full information about Japan, including missionary work there.

DATTA, SURENDRA K. The Desire of India. pp. 307. 1908. Student Christian Movement. $1.00. Missionary Education Movement. 35 cents, 50 cents.

A satisfactory account of India as a mission field; written by a clever Indian Christian.

DENNIS, JAMES S. The New Horoscope of Missions. pp. 248. 1908. Revell. $1 00.

A course of lectures on modern aspects of the foreign missionary question, by one of the world's foremost missionary authorities.

DENNIS, JAMES S. Social Evils in the Non-Christian World. pp. 172. S. V. M. Out of print.

Reprinted from Volume I of "Christian Missions and Social Progress," excellent expositions in concise form of social conditions in mission lands; shows utter inadequacy of non-Christian religions to meet or to solve these problems.

DWIGHT, HENRY O, TUPPER, H. A, JR., BLISS, E. M. The Enclyclopedia of Missions. pp. 851. 1904. Funk & Wagnalls. $6.00.

A most useful volume covering almost every phase of missions, being descriptive, historical, biographical, and statistical; best volume of the sort in the English language.

EDWARDS, MARTIN R. The Work of the Medical Missionary. pp. 65. 1909. S. V. M. 20 cents.

A guide, with ample references, to the study of the various phases of this subject.

FORSYTH, P. T. Missions in State and Church. pp 344. 1908. Doran. $1.75.

Missionary sermons and addresses by one of the most vigorous minds in the British pulpit.

GALE, JAMES S. Korea in Transition. pp. 269. 1909. Missionary Education Movement. 35 cents, 50 cents.

Gives an insight into present Korean conditions, including Christian revival, and into the Korean mind and character.

GRIFFIS, WILLIAM E. Verbeck of Japan. pp. 376. 1900. Revell. $1.50.

Story of the foundation work done for Christian missions in Japan by Guido Fridolin Verbeck.

GORDON, A. J. The Holy Spirit in Missions. pp. 241. 1893. Revell. 50 cents, $1 25.

Emphasizes the special significance and errand of missions, and discusses the place of the Divine Spirit in the enterprise.

JESSUP, HENRY H. Fifty-three Years in Syria. 2 vols pp. 404; 429. 1910. Revell $5 00.

Inspiring biography; informing account of the progress of the Gospel in the land of its birth.

JEVONS, FRANK B. Introduction to the Study of Comparative Religion. pp. 283. 1908. Macmillan $1.50.

The first book to be read by any one who purposes to make a study of comparative religion.

JONES, JOHN P. India: Its Life and Thought. pp. 448. 1908. Macmillan. $2.50.

Deals mainly with the religious beliefs and the new trends of thought in India, written by a recognized authority.

KELLOGG, S. H. A Handbook of Comparative Religion. pp. 185. 1905 S. V. M. 30 cents, 75 cents.

A brief, comparative study of the various great religions in their main teachings, written by one who has had years of contact with some of these faiths on the mission field.

LAWRENCE, EDWARD A. Introduction to the Study of Foreign Missions. pp. 143. 1901. S V. M. 25 cents, 40 cents.

Constitutes the permanently valuable portions of the larger volume, "Modern Missions in the East."

McKENZIE, F. A. The Unveiled East. pp. 347. 1907. Dutton. $3.50.

Thoughtful discussion, by a well-known journalist, of Far Eastern problems.

MENZIES, ALLAN. History of Religion. pp. 438. 1895. Scribner $1.50.

A compendious view of ancient and present-day religions from the modern standpoint.

MILLIGAN, R. H The Jungle Folk of Africa. pp. 380. 1908. Revell. $1 50.

Fresh, vivid descriptions; illuminates the study of missionary effort in the interior of Africa.

MORRISON, JOHN. New Ideas in India. pp. 282. 1907. Macmillan. $1 60.

A careful account of the new social and religious movements in India, by an experienced Scotch missionary educator in Calcutta.

MOTT, JOHN R. The Evangelization of the World in This Generation. pp. 245. 1900. S. V M. 35 cents, $1.00.

A statement of the Church's missionary obligation to the present generation of non-Christians, surveys the field, enumerates the difficulties, reviews previous missionary successes of the Church, and examines her resources with reference to the evangelizing of the world in this generation; one of the most influential books in modern missionary literature, written by a well-known missionary leader and author.

MOTT, JOHN R. The Pastor and Modern Missions. pp. 249. 1904. S. V. M 35 cents, $1.00.

A study of the position of the pastor as leader in the missionary enterprise; includes a masterly survey of world conditions at the opening of the century; valuable material for sermons and addresses.

MUIR, WILLIAM. The Call of the New Era. pp. 351. 1910. American Tract Society $1 25. Morgan & Scott. 6s. (One of the Morgan & Scott Missionary series.)

Gives a trustworthy account of missionary history beginning in the era of preparation for Christ and closing in the summons to every Christian of the present era, reveals a scholarly, accurate and spiritual reading of missionary history, written by a Scottish minister, and has a special message to ministers.

MURRAY, ANDREW. The Key to the Missionary Problem. pp 204 1901. American Tract Society. 75 cents.

Unequalled as indicating the place of prayer in solving the missionary problem.

MURRAY, J. LOVELL. The Apologetic of Modern Missions. pp. 97. Revised 1911. S. V. M. 25 cents.

An outline study in the defense of Christian missions against current criticisms; contains references to arsenals both of attack and defense

NAYLOR, WILSON S. Daybreak in the Dark Continent. pp. 315. Revised 1912. Missionary Education Movement. 35 cents, 50 cents.

Best text-book on Africa as a mission field; bulk of treatment given to Central Africa.

PATON, JAMES, editor. Autobiography of John G. Paton. pp. 481. 1907. Revell. $1.50

One of the greatest volumes of missionary biography, life of the famous missionary to the New Hebrides, edited by his brother.

REPORT OF CONFERENCE OF THE WORLD'S STUDENT CHRISTIAN FEDERATION, CONSTANTINOPLE 1911. pp. 324. 1911. W. S. C. F. 35 cents.

Reveals progress of the Student Christian Movements of the world.

RICHARDS, E. H., and OTHERS. Religions of Mission Fields as Viewed by Protestant Missionaries pp. 300. 1905. S. V. M. 35 cents, 50 cents.

Brief accounts of the ten great religions of the mission countries of the world, written by missionaries who have been in long and intimate contact with them.

ROSS, E. A. The Changing Chinese pp. 356. 1911. Century Company. $2.40.

A mass of reliable information, much of it first hand, about China and her people and the present transformations in the Empire; given in sparkling style by a distinguished sociologist; contains a valuable chapter on missions; finely illustrated.

SINKER, ROBERT. Memorials of the Honorable Ion Keith-Falconer. pp. 258. 1903. Deighton, Bell. $1.85.

Best account of the brief but remarkable career of the young Scottish nobleman who pioneered Christian missions in Arabia.

SMITH, ARTHUR H. China and America Today. pp. 256. 1907. Revell. $1.25.

Account of relations past and present between these two countries; America's new responsibilities for peace and progress around the Pacific basin.

SMITH, ARTHUR H. China in Convulsion. 2 vols. pp. 364; 406. 1901. Revell $5.00.

Standard work on the Boxer Uprising.

SMITH, GEORGE. The Life of William Carey, D.D. pp. 389. 1887 John Murray. 7s. 6d.

Best life of the pioneer of nineteenth century missions.

SPEER, ROBERT E. Christianity and the Nations pp. 399. 1910. Revell. $2.00.

The Duff Lectures for 1910; treat of a variety of missionary questions, both theoretical and practical; no other one volume gives so compactly an understanding of the basis, purpose, problems, message, bearings, and influence of Christian missions; written by one of the best-known missionary experts and apologists

SPEER, ROBERT E. South American Problems. pp. 256. 1912. S. V M. 50 cents, 75 cents.

The latest text-book on South America, covers the present economic, educational, moral and religious conditions in South America, and deals outspokenly, but sympathetically, with the problems of the hour, highly informing and authoritative.

SPEER, ROBERT E. The Light of the World. pp 372. 1911. Macmillan. 35 cents, 50 cents.

A valuable text-book on comparative religion, fair and considerate in its treatment of the great non-Christian faiths, while loyal to Christianity as God's supreme and unique revelation, abounds in quotations from competent authorities.

STUDENTS AND THE PRESENT MISSIONARY CRISIS. pp 600. 1910 S V. M. $1.50.

Addresses given at the Rochester Convention of the Student Volunteer Movement; a mine of information and illumination.

STUNTZ, HOMER C. The Philippines and the Far East. pp. 514. 1904. Jennings & Graham. $1 75.

A survey, historical, racial, political, and religious, of conditions in the Philippines; gives an account of the Protestant missionary effort now being carried on; written by a missionary who had unusual opportunities for investigation

TAYLOR, MRS HOWARD. Pastor Hsi: Confucian Scholar and Christian. pp. 494. 1907. China Inland Mission. $1.50.

A miracle of modern missions; combines the two former volumes, "One of China's Scholars" and "Pastor Hsi, One of China's Christians."

UNDERWOOD, HORACE G. The Call of Korea pp. 204. 1908. Revell. 35 cents, 75 cents.

Full of interesting information; shows Korea as a dead-ripe mission field.

WARNECK, JOH. The Living Christ and Dying Heathenism. pp. 312. 1909. Revell. $1.75.

A scientific exposition of animism by a German scholar and missionary, a revelation of the desperate needs of paganism and of the Gospel's supreme power to transform and uplift whole races.

WARNECK, GUSTAV. Outline of a History of Protestant Missions pp. 364. 1901. Revell. $2.80.

A reliable history of missions by one of Germany's foremost missionary authorities.

WELLS, JAMES. Stewart of Lovedale. pp. 419. 1909. Revell. $1.50

Life story of one of Africa's greatest statesmen missionaries.

WELSH, R. E. The Challenge to Christian Missions. pp. 188. 1902. Allenson. 30 cents, $1.00.

A discriminating exposition and defense of Christian missions.

WHERRY, E. M., ZWEMER, S. M., and MYLREA, C. G., editors Islam and Missions. pp. 298. 1911 Revell. $1.50.

Nothing will so satisfactorily bring one up to date on the Mohammedan situation to-day, both in its political and religious aspects, as this collection of the papers read at the recent Lucknow Conference on Missions to Moslems.

WISHARD, JOHN G. Twenty Years in Persia pp. 344 1908 Revell. $1 50

Replete with first-hand information on Persia and missionary work there; throws light on the reform movements now in progress in that country.

ZWEMER, SAMUEL M. Arabia: The Cradle of Islam. pp. 437 1900 Revell. $2.00.

Best volume on the Arabian peninsula; written by a pioneer missionary of unusual ability, both to see and to relate.

ZWEMER, SAMUEL M. Islam: A Challenge to Faith. pp. 295. 1907. S. V M 35 cents, $1 00.

An exposition of the practice, ethics and ritual of Mohammedanism, by a leading authority, account of the rise and spread of the faith and its present conditions.

ZWEMER, SAMUEL M., and BROWN, ARTHUR J.: The Nearer and Farther East. pp 325. 1908 Macmillan. 35 cents, 50 cents.

A survey of missionary conditions in Moslem lands and in Korea, Siam, and Burma.

A LIST OF BOOKS ON EDUCATION FOR MISSIONARY CANDIDATES

This list has been prepared by Dr. T. H. P. Sailer. A very few books to serve as the beginning of a personal library are marked **; other books that may be of special interest are marked *.

EDUCATION AND THE CHRISTIANIZATION OF NATIONAL LIFE

** EDUCATION IN RELATION TO THE CHRISTIANIZATION OF NATIONAL LIFE. Report of Commission III of the Edinburgh World Conference. pp. 471. 1910. Revell. 75 cents.

The most thorough discussion in print of the problems of educational missions. Testimony is given from numerous correspondents all over the world as to the aims and problems of educational work. The relation of Christian truth to indigenous thought and feeling, industrial training and the training of teachers occupy three chapters. The need of a broad and thorough understanding of educational principles by prospective missionaries is strongly urged. The whole discussion is on a high plane and is exceedingly stimulating.

KINDERGARTEN

*BLOW, SUSAN E. Educational Influences in the Kindergarten. pp. 386. 1908. Appleton. $1.50.

An interesting discussion of four tendencies in recent kindergarten work, the correlation tendency of the Herbartians, the free-play tendency of Stanley Hall's school, the industrial tendency of John Dewey, and the stricter Froebelian interpretation. The first three are criticized from the standpoint of the fourth

BLOW, SUSAN E. Mottoes and Commentaries of Froebel's Mother Play. pp. 272. 1895. Appleton. $1.50.

*BLOW, SUSAN E. Symbolic Education. pp. 251. 1894. Appleton. $1 50.

Miss Blow is an enthusiastic interpreter of the philosophy of Froebel. She here presents the main principles on which his kindergarten work is based. The style is philosophical, but animated.

HARRISON, ELIZABETH. A Study of Child Nature. pp. 207. 1890 Chicago Kindergarten College. $1.00.

Helpful suggestions on the training of children in the home and kindergarten, with illustrations from actual experience.

HUGHES, J. L. Froebel's Educational Laws for All Teachers. pp. 206. 1897. Appleton. $1.50

An enthusiastic presentation of Froebel's ideals, which are so needed in the training of the Orient. Froebel has suffered much from only partial understanding and application of his principles. The fundamental ideas of unity and self-activity are reiterated and contrasted with the ideas of other systems Concrete methods are not described.

SONGS AND MUSIC OF FROEBEL'S MOTHER PLAY. pp. 316. 1895. Appleton. $1.50.

Miss Blow has translated into clear English the commentary on Froebel's Mother Play and added free poetic renderings of the mottoes. The second volume contains the songs in free translations with new and appropriate music. Froebel's original illustrations are retained.

WIGGIN, K. D., and SMITH, N. A. The Republic of Childhood. 3 vols., with titles, Froebel's Gifts, Froebel's Occupations, and Kindergarten Principles and Practice. pp. 202; 313; 205. 1896. Houghton, Mifflin. $1.00 each.

In the first two volumes a chapter is devoted to each of Froebel's gifts and occupations, with comments on the principles involved. The third volume discusses general kindergarten principles. The style is simple and there are many practical suggestions derived from experience, but no detailed programme worked out.

ELEMENTARY SCHOOL

*DEWEY, JOHN. The Child and the Curriculum. pp. 40. 1902. University of Chicago Press. 25 cents.

An essay on the theory of the relation of the subject matter of study to the developing child. It presents more acute and original thinking than the average educational treatise of ten times its length. The necessity of presenting the subject matter in terms of the child's own understanding and impulses is clearly shown.

**DEWEY, JOHN. The School and Society. pp 129. 1900. University of Chicago Press. $1.00.

A series of lectures by the leading American philosopher of education, describing the principles on which the University Elementary School is conducted. The thesis maintained is that the school should be more closely connected with the needs of society. The lectures contain some far-reaching truths and have had an influence on educational thought out of all proportion to their bulk.

*DEWEY, JOHN. The School and the Child pp. 127. 1906. Blackie & Son, London. 1s.

A reprint of the preceding essay, together with eight articles written originally by Dr. Dewey for the *Elementary School Record*, and now out of print. The latter articles treat fundamental principles in the work of the elementary school, such as the psychology of occupations, the aim of history in the elementary school, etc.

DOPP, KATHARINE. The Place of the Industries in Elementary Education. pp. 270. 1905. University of Chicago Press. $1.00.

Based on the ideas presented by Dr. Dewey in *The School and Society*. Discusses the significance of each of the industrial epochs for education and indicates applications to the development of the child. The theoretical discussion is very thoughtful and will be more valuable to most teachers than the suggested lessons based on New England history.

McMURRY, C. A. Course of Study in the Eight Grades. 2 vols. pp. 236; 226. 1906. Macmillan. 75 cents each.

A list of topics to be taken up in the various studies of the elementary school is presented, together with text-books and reference books for the teacher. Methods are suggested, but the principal emphasis is upon subject matter. The needs of the American school are, of course, in mind.

*McMURRY, C. A. The Elements of General Method pp. 331. 1903. Macmillan. (Revised edition.) 90 cents.

A plain and practical treatment of the principles underlying elementary education, such as the moral aim, discrimination of the relative value of studies, interest, correlation, etc. The standpoint is that of the Herbartian school. The author is not strikingly original, but straightforward and sane.

*McMURRY, C. A., and F. M. The Method of the Recitation. pp 339. 1903. Macmillan. (Revised edition.) 90 cents.

Based on the preceding, it works out the application of the five formal Herbartian steps to elementary teaching. Perhaps the best general introduction to the principles of teaching for the beginner to read.

**McMURRY, F. M. How to Study and Teaching How to Study. pp. 324. 1909. Houghton, Mifflin. $1.25.

A book that every teacher should own and digest. Teaching in most of our schools would be revolutionized and manifolded in value if the recommendations of this book were carried out. Few things are more important than learning how to study, and few things are more neglected by the average teacher.

** THE ELEMENTARY SCHOOL CURRICULUM. pp. 526. 1908. Teachers' College. $2.00.

A bound reprint of five numbers of the *Teachers' College Record*, treating the work of the seven grades of the Horace Mann Elementary School, one of the best elementary schools in the United States. The book should be of great value to any elementary teacher who wishes specific suggestions on the curriculum and the ideals and general methods of teaching the subjects.

WINTERBURN, ROSA V. Methods in Teaching. pp. 355. 1909. Macmillan. $1.25.

Suggestions of detailed methods for teaching English, arithmetic, nature study, history, etc., in the elementary grades are offered. Many of the sections are written by the teachers of these subjects in the various grades. Similar in idea to the preceding book, but briefer and with much less space given to manual training and art.

TEACHING OF SPECIAL SUBJECTS

BAHLSEN, L. The Teaching of Modern Languages. pp. 97. 1905. Ginn. 50 cents.

Based on the reform methods introduced in Germany by Vietor. The suggestions are useful for those teaching any language.

BOURNE, H. E. The Teaching of History and Civics. pp. 385. 2d edition, with bibliographies revised. 1910.

CARPENTER, BAKER and SCOTT. The Teaching of English. pp. 380. 1903.

LLOYD and BIGELOW. The Teaching of Biology. pp. 491. 1904.

SMITH & HALL. The Teaching of Chemistry and Physics. pp. 377. 1904. American Teachers' Series. Longmans. $1.50 each.

These four books are designed primarily to meet the needs of the secondary school teacher. Both subject matter and methods of presentation are treated, but the former naturally occupies more space than in books on elementary school work. The first on the list has a chapter on work in the grades. There are good bibliographies on reference and text-books, principles and methods of teaching. The series includes also books on the teaching of mathematics and of classics. The publishers expect to bring the bibliographies up to date as new editions are issued.

HODGE, C. F. Nature Study and Life pp. 514. 1902. Ginn. $1.50.

The author argues for nature study from the standpoint of the natural interests and uses of the child as opposed to those of the scientist He shows how to help the American child to appreciate his physical surroundings.

HOLTZ, F. L. Nature Study. pp. 546. 1908. Scribner. $1.50.

Presents first the motives and principles underlying nature study, then gives a chapter on each of the fields to be entered by the elementary school, and finally a list of topics for study in the eight grades. It has the inevitable disadvantage of being based on American conditions, but from that standpoint represents the most recent thought on the subject.

*HUEY, E. B. The Psychology and Pedagogy of Reading. pp. 469. 1908. Macmillan. $1.40.

The first part, on the psychology of reading, is somewhat technical. The second part is historical. The remainder of the book, on the pedagogy and hygiene of reading, is extremely suggestive, and should be read by all those who have to teach children. The author believes that reading is usually taught too early and by unwise methods. His recommendations are based on careful scientific study.

McMURRY, C. A. Special Method in Reading in the Grades. 1909. Macmillan. $1.25.

SPECIAL METHOD IN HISTORY. pp .291. 1903. 75 cents.

SPECIAL METHOD IN GEOGRAPHY. pp. 217. 1903. 70 cents.

SPECIAL METHOD IN ARITHMETIC. pp. 225. 1905. 70 cents.

SPECIAL METHOD IN ELEMENTARY SCIENCE. pp. 275. 1905. 75 cents.

Like the other books by McMurry, these are plain and practical, without being highly original in either style or treatment. They are especially adapted to American surroundings.

SMITH, D. E. The Teaching of Elementary Mathematics. . pp. 312. 1900. Macmillan. $1 00.

Covers the teaching of arithmetic, algebra and geometry, giving in each case a sketch of the growth of the subject, the reasons for teaching it, and methods to be followed. Less detailed for elementary arithmetic than McMurry, but written with a wider outlook.

GENERAL THEORY OF EDUCATION

BAGLEY, W. C. The Educative Process. pp. 358. 1905. Macmillan. $1.25.

Discusses the biological, logical and psychological bases of education. An excellent introduction for one who wishes to see education in the large as the acquisition of individual experience. It should be supplemented by a book which treats the social phases of education.

*BUBBERLY, E. P. Changing Conceptions of Education. pp. 70. 1909. Houghton, Mifflin. 35 cents.

The author shows how, in response to the needs of life, the conception of education has changed from that of a transmission of the accumulated traditions of society, through one of psychological adaptation to the needs of the individual, to the sociological one of an instrument of democracy to meet the needs of democracy. The discussion is clear and vigorous.

CARLETON, F. T. Education and Industrial Evolution. pp. 320. 1908. Macmillan. $1.25.

A plea for the adaptation of the school to the present needs of the bulk of society The school has been adjusted mainly to the needs of the few who look forward to professional life rather than to those of the many who must be industrial wage-earners. The discussion is vigorous and stimulating.

DAVENPORT, E. Education for Efficiency. pp. 184. 1909. Heath. $1.00.

A series of spirited addresses. The writer holds that one-fourth of the time of all education should be devoted to vocational work, that industrial education must be developed for the ninety-five per cent of our population who do not enter professional life, and that this must be conducted in such a way as to retain its graduates in the industries.

*DEWEY, JOHN. Ethical Principles Underlying Education. pp. 34. 1903. University of Chicago Press. 25 cents.

Holds that the aim of the school is to develop a broad social morality, and that the value of studies is measured by their contributions to social insight, social responsiveness and social initiative.

*DEWEY, JOHN. The Educational Situation. pp. 104. 1902. University of Chicago Press. 50 cents.

Three chapters on the work of the elementary school, the secondary school and the college The thesis is that educational theory in response to social needs has advanced further than practice. The present dislocation is shown and the principles by which adjustment is to be secured are indicated. No educators more than missionaries need to study the problems of educational adjustment to social conditions.

ELIOT, C W. Education for Efficiency. pp. 58. 1909. Houghton, Mifflin. 35 cents.

Two addresses in President Eliot's trenchant style in which he contends for the development of initiative, enthusiasm and practical efficiency, which are too often not even sought in traditional education. We are still far from realizing fully the ideals which Dr. Eliot has advocated for so many years.

ELIOT, C. W. Educational Reform. pp. 418. 1898. Century Company. $2.00.

Addresses delivered at various times by the man who has perhaps done more than any other to destroy antiquated ideals in American education. President Eliot's style is most incisive, and when we agree with him it is safe to say that we have our arguments in the most vigorous form in which they could be put. Many of these problems of American education will repeat themselves on the foreign field.

HARRIS, W. T. Psychologic Foundations of Education. pp. 400. 1898. Appleton. $1.50.

A philosophical discussion containing some very acute and suggestive things. The functions of the mind and the necessary implications of thought are presented from the standpoint of a Christian metaphysics. The third part treats the relation of institutions, art, etc., to education The book is not all easy reading, but to some types of mind it will be most fascinating.

HUGHES, R. E. The Making of Citizens. pp. 405 1902. Scribner. $1.50.

A comparative study of the primary and secondary school systems of Great Britain, France, Germany and the United States, with chapters on the education of girls and defectives. The book makes a good introduction for those who wish to learn the main educational trends in the four countries mentioned. Those who wish to study this subject more in detail should consult Russell's German Higher Schools and Farrington's Public Primary School System of France, and French Secondary Schools.

O'SHEA, M. V. Education as Adjustment. pp. 317. 1905. Longmans. $1.50.

A thoughtful discussion of education considered as adjustment to the individual and social environment The biological and psychological bases of education are emphasized rather than methods of teaching.

O'SHEA, M. V. Dynamic Factors in Education. pp. 320. 1906. Macmillan. $1 25

The author shows the significance of the restlessness of children, and criticizes the average school as requiring too much physical restraint. He advocates more of manual activity in education. He indicates sources of unnecessary fatigue and nervous strain.

ROWE, S. H. Habit Formation and the Science of Teaching. pp. 308. 1909. Longmans. $1.50.

An important but much neglected subject. The author gives a broad definition to the term habit, and traces it in fields where it is often not recognized.

SNEDDEN, DAVID. The Problem of Vocational Education pp 86. 1910. Houghton, Mifflin. 35 cents.

The writer, who has recently become Commissioner of Education for Massachusetts, is one of our more acute students of educational principles. He shows the present need of vocational education by the school, since the home and the shop are no longer able to meet the demands, and also the changes necessary in the administration of the schools The relation of vocational to liberal education is discussed

SOCIAL EDUCATION

BAGLEY, W. C. Classroom Management. pp. 322. 1907. Macmillan. $1.25

The writer emphasizes the mechanical rather than the inspirational side of teaching He stresses drill and habit and methods for the mass. The book will be useful for those who are unsystematic in their work.

DUTTON, S T, and SNEDDEN, DAVID. The Administration of Public Education in the United States. pp. 601. 1908. Macmillan. $1.75.

A review of the broad field of public education in the United States. An excellent introduction to the study of our national system. While details and statistics are freely cited, they are accompanied by thoughtful comments of principles and tendencies which should be considered by those working in all fields

ELIOT, C. W. University Administration. pp 266. 1908 Houghton, Mifflin. $1.50.

The problems of Harvard University are in many ways different from those of colleges under the care of missionaries, but much of President Eliot's vigorous common sense will be found useful to the administrator. The subjects treated are university trustees, alumni, faculty, elective system, methods of instruction and social organization.

**GILBERT, C. B. The School and Its Life. pp. 259. 1906. Silver, Burdett & Co. $1.25.

School management from the standpoint of the principal. A very stimulating discussion based on up-to-date educational theory. Every missionary school principal should read this book. It is neither wooden nor overloaded with details irrelevant to the missionary.

JOHNSON, G. E. Education by Plays and Games. pp. 234. 1907. Ginn. $1.10.

Three chapters on the meaning of play, its importance in education, and the characteristics of the periods of childhood are followed by a full list of plays for each age, with brief descriptions.

REEDER, R. R. How 200 Children Live and Learn. pp. 247. 1909. New York Charities Publishing Committee. $1.25.

An account, by the superintendent, of the work of the New York Orphan Asylum. Everything possible is done to prevent the usual deadening effects of institutional life and instead to foster individual initiative and character. There are excellent, though brief, chapters on moral and religious training and on personal touch. The book will be most suggestive and stimulating to one who has to supervise a boarding school.

*SCOTT, C. A. Social Education. pp. 300. 1908. Ginn. $1.25.

A discussion of a phase of education that has been too often neglected. The book is suggestive rather than systematic It should broaden the methods of the average teacher.

SHAW, E. R. School Hygiene. pp. 260. 1901. Macmillan. $1.00.

This has been for some years one of the standard treatments of the subject. The principal topics presented are the arrangement of the rooms, buildings and grounds, heating, ventilation and sanitation, furniture and hygienic methods of work. Those with limited funds at their disposal will not be able to carry out all the suggestions.

SNEDDEN and ALLEN. School Reports and School Efficiency. pp. 183. 1908. Macmillan. $1.50.

After brief introductory chapters, a long list of the most significant school reports of American cities is presented with comments. Many additional questions are suggested and profitable ways of condensing statistics. Those who have oversight of schools would probably get helpful suggestions for reports, even where conditions dealt with are quite different from those of American cities.

WOOD, T. D. Health and Education pp. 110. 1910. University of Chicago Press. 75 cents.

An excellent summary of recent thought on the subject of health examinations, school sanitation, the hygiene of instruction, health instruction and physical education. Free play in the open air, involving interesting and natural activity, is recommended, as opposed to formal drills in the gymnasium.

CHILD STUDY

*KIRKPATRICK, E. A. Essentials of Child Study. pp. 384. 1903. Macmillan. $1.25.

The best introduction for one who wishes to make a scientific study of child nature The development of the various instincts characteristic of childhood are discussed in some detail, and brief suggestions made for the educator. At the end of each chapter are questions and references for further study.

*O'SHEA, M. V. Social Development and Education. pp. 561. 1909. Houghton, Mifflin. $2.00.

The first part of the book is a study of the typical social attitudes of children, sociability, sense of duty and justice, docility, resentment, etc. The second part discusses methods of social training. The book is full of material valuable both to the teacher and the parent, and deserves careful study by those who consider themselves responsible for the best development of character.

ROWE, S. H. The Physical Nature of the Child. pp. 211. 1899. Macmillan. 90 cents.

Discusses tests for defective faculties, treatment for nervousness and fatigue, the conditions of adolescence and proper physical surroundings for the school and the home.

TANNER, AMY. The Child. pp. 430. 1904. Rand, McNally. $1.25.

Another excellent introduction to child study, written from the standpoint of somewhat more personal interest in the child than Kirkpatrick's book. A useful supplement to the latter.

ADOLESCENCE

BUCK, WINIFRED. Boys' Self-Governing Clubs. pp. 218. 1903. Macmillan. 50 cents.

The experience of a worker with Boys' Clubs on the East Side of New York City. It should be helpful to those who have to deal with boys outside of school hours, a period the importance of which is becoming increasingly recognized. There are wise suggestions as to the limits of self-government.

*FORBUSH, W. B. The Boy Problem. pp. 219. 1907. 6th edition (revised). Pilgrim Press. $1.00.

The best book for those who have to deal with boys. Treats work in both church and home, and describes many organizations and devices, but exalts personal influence as supremely effective. At the end of each chapter is a select bibliography.

*HALL, G. STANLEY. Adolescence. 2 vols. pp. 589; 784. 1904. Appleton. $7.50.

President Hall has emptied into these two volumes the contents of many note books. He writes in a glowing style of the physical and mental characteristics of adolescence. To many of his statements and theories, exceptions will be taken, but no student of the subject can afford to neglect President Hall's great learning and vigorous thought.

*HALL, G. STANLEY. Youth. pp. 379 1906. Appleton. $1.50.

A condensation of the preceding, the chapters especially bearing on education having been selected. For a student with plenty of time, the larger work would be distinctly preferable, but a busy person can here get President Hall's viewpoint and most important mateial.

EDUCATIONAL PSYCHOLOGY

*DEWEY, JOHN. How We Think pp. 224. 1910. Heath. $1.00.

A discussion of reflective or purposive thinking in Dr. Dewey's usual clear and thorough style. He distinguishes five steps in reasoning and indicates the true functions of induction and deduction, of analysis and synthesis. Practical applications of value are made to the work of the teacher. Dr. Dewey's own thinking is fundamental, his distinctions and illustrations are clear. As an educational theorist he has few, if any, equals.

*DEWEY, JOHN. Interest as Related to Will. pp. 40. 1899. University of Chicago Press. 25 cents.

A fundamental discussion. Not easy reading and not to be grasped at a sitting by the average person, but well worth careful study. Dr Dewey has furnished many writers on education with their principal ideas.

HECK, W. H. Mental Discipline. pp. 208. 2d edition, revised. 1911. John Lane. $1.00.

For a number of years there has been a strong reaction against the view that the criterion of the value of the subject was its difficulty rather than its content. It is claimed that the so-called disciplinary value of certain subjects is transferable to other subjects in only a very slight degree. While inclining to the more recent view, the author presents a useful summary of the discussion of the subject by various writers.

*JAMES, WILLIAM. Talks to Teachers. pp. 301. 1899. Holt. $1.50.

A series of popular lectures on the application of psychological principles to teaching in Professor James' brilliant style. Specific methods could hardly be inferred from this book by the inexperienced teacher, but there is much to stimulate. No one has ever put certain maxims of character formation more incisively.

LANGE, K. Apperception. pp. 279. 1893. Heath. $1.00.

No doctrine has had more influence on methods of instruction than that of apperception as developed by the Hebartians. While the psychology on which it rests has been in some ways superseded, most of its practical application is still valid and valuable. Lange's book is a thorough discussion.

MÜNSTERBERG, HUGO Psychology and the Teacher. pp. 330. 1909. Appleton. $1.50.

Less brilliant than Professor James' book, but more detailed, systematic and up-to-date Some of the recent educational theories are questioned by the writer.

THORNDIKE, E. L. Educational Psychology. pp. 248. 2d edition revised, and enlarged. 1910. Teachers' College. $1.50.

An attempt to apply quantitative measurement to the psychological differences of individuals. Investigations of the influence of sex, ancestry and environment are summarized and discussed. Many common suppositions are shown to be without scientific basis. The book is somewhat technical in character, and the results as a whole are rather negative, but the subject is one which will probably undergo considerable development.

*THORNDIKE, E. L. Principles of Teaching. pp. 273. 1906. Seiler. $1.25.

Treats briefly the various psychological facts involved in teaching, then the application of these to teaching, and finally offers a number of practical problems, some of which are very suggestive. The center of interest is in the psychology of the pupil rather than in the subject matter.

STORY TELLING

BRYANT, SARA C. How to Tell Stories to Children. pp. 260. 1905. Houghton, Mifflin. $1.00.

An introduction on the purpose of story telling, the qualities of narrative that children most like, and hints for the adaptation of stories for telling, with a collection of short stories adapted for oral use in the first five grades. The selection and style are both excellent.

BRYANT, SARA C. Stories to Tell Children. pp. 243. 1907. Houghton, Mifflin. $1.00.

A second series of stories arranged for telling. The introduction is brief, and most of the book is given to the tales, which are for the most part exceedingly good.

HERVEY, W. C. Picture Work. pp. 91. 1896. Revell. 30 cents.

A very suggestive booklet on the art of illustration and story telling in teaching. The hints are concise and well arranged. The treatment has long been one of the best of its kind.

ST. JOHN, E. P. Stories and Story Telling. pp. 100. 1910. Pilgrim Press. 50 cents.

The essential value of the story for moral training is found in its appeal to the emotions; excellent suggestions are given for improvement in the art of story telling. Especially good is the chapter on the use of stories as determined by their aim. The little book is well worth reading by those who have the moral training of children in hand.

RELIGIOUS EDUCATION

BURTON, E. D., and MATHEWS, SHAILER. Principles and Ideals of the Sunday School. pp 207. 1903 University of Chicago Press. $1.00.

Written by two theological professors with practical experience in Sunday School work. The main interest is in the intelligent presentation and understanding of the Bible. The responsibility of the pastor for the work of teaching is strongly emphasized.

CHAMBERLIN, G. L. Introduction to the Bible. pp. 206. 1904. University of Chicago Press. $1.00.

A course of forty lessons for children from 9 to 10 years of age, intended to give a general knowledge of the contents and teachings of the Bible "akin to a mechanic's knowledge and love of his tools." As a whole, far in advance of most of our Sunday School material.

CHAMBERLIN, G. L., and KERN, M. R. Child Religion in Song and Story. Manual for Teacher. pp. 252. 1907. University of Chicago Press. $1.25.

A series of thirty-nine lessons for children from 6 to 9 years of age. Special note books to accompany the manual cost 40 cents each. The stories have no chronological sequence, but are grouped around simple ideas, such as honor to parents, the Heavenly Father, joy in giving, etc. American children are presupposed, but the manual should offer valuable suggestions to missionaries. A second series has been issued to cover another year of the same grade.

*COE, G. A. Education in Religion and Morals. pp. 434. 1904. Revell. $1.35.

Defines education as the effort to assist in development toward social adjustment and efficiency. Shows the implications of this viewpoint for religion. Discusses the periods of individual development and the share of the family, school and church in religious education. An excellent book for those who wish to see the question in the large.

COE, G. A. The Spiritual Life. pp. 279. 1900. Revell. $1.00.

A study of religion from the psychological standpoint, showing the effect of temperament, of various adolescent traits, and of suggestibility. The author claims that our conceptions of spirituality have been unduly feminized.

FERRIS, C. S. The Sunday Kindergarten. pp. 271. 1909. University of Chicago Press. $1.25.

A series of forty-three lessons worked out in detail. Kindergarten methods are employed, but trained kindergartners are not necessary to carry them out. Plays, stories and constructive work are suggested for each lesson, and music given for a number of the plays as well as for opening and closing exercises. Some kindergarten equipment is very desirable, but the most essential parts could probably be improvised without great difficulty.

GATES, H. W. The Life of Jesus. Teachers' Manual. pp. 156. 1906. University of Chicago Press. 75 cents.

Forty-two lessons for children of from 10 to 13 years of age. A number of references to other books accompany each copy, with hints on preparation and suggestions for teaching. Special note books for pupils cost 50 cents each, but could be dispensed with. The treatment is thoughtful, but not strikingly original.

HASLETT, S. B. A Pedagogical Bible School pp. 383. 1903. Revell. $1.25.

Shows the growth of the Sunday School and its methods. Devotes several chapters to a discussion of the characteristics of childhood and of adolescence. Lays down principles for a curriculum and outlines topics for the different grades. More of discussion than in the book by Pease, and less on the curriculum and on specific methods.

JENKS, J. W. Social Significance of the Teachings of Jesus. pp. 168. 1906. Association Press. 50 cents, 75 cents.

A series of lessons arranged for daily study with questions for class discussion at the end of each week. The day's work consists of readings from the Bible and from reference books, and to these are added helpful comments by the author. The spirit is earnest and thoughtful. The Association Press has other textbooks modeled on the same lines.

MCKINLEY, C. E. Educational Evangelism. pp. 265. 1905. Pilgrim Press. $1.25.

The changing nature of the individual in the transition to adolescence is well presented. The book is written from the standpoint of a pastor.

**PEASE, G. A. Outline of a Bible School Curriculum. pp. 418. 1904. University of Chicago Press. $1.50.

A most useful and suggestive book. Treats first the characteristics of each period of development from the kindergarten to the adult stage; then outlines a curriculum for every Sunday in the year, and gives several specimen lessons and a bibliography in connection with each year. The book indicates in general the position toward which the best Bible study is moving.

* PROCEEDINGS OF THE CONVENTIONS OF THE RELIGIOUS EDUCATION ASSOCIATION, 5 vols pp. 422; 640; 525; 379; 319. 1903, 1904, 1905, 1907, 1908 Now sold for 75 cents, $1.00, $1.00, $1.00 and $1 50 respectively.

Reports of addresses on all phases of religious education by many speakers. These necessarily vary much in quality, but some of them are of great importance. The titles of the last four volumes are: "The Bible in Practical Life," "The Aims of Religious Education," "The Materials of Religious Education," "Education and National Character."

RUGH, C. E., and OTHERS. Moral Training in Public Schools. pp. 203. 1907. Ginn. $1.50.

Five essays selected as the best of those submitted in competition for a prize. The first presents very clearly the viewpoint of the party that holds that morals should be taught by affording occasions for moral activity rather than by precept.

*SADLER, M. E., editor Moral Instruction and Training in Schools. 2 vols. pp. 538; 378. 1908. Longmans. $1.50 each.

A series of papers in response to an inquiry on the subject of moral education in schools. Vol. I treats replies from Great Britain, and Vol. II those from the colonies and from other countries.

SLATTERY, MARGARET. Talks to the Training Class. pp. 84. 1906. Pilgrim Press. 25 cents, 60 cents

Popular and helpful chapters on child nature and the best methods of treating it in teaching. The intense sympathy of the writer is a stimulus, and the illustrations from life will be more suggestive to the beginner than any amount of abstract definitions.

PERSONAL DEVELOPMENT

GULICK, LUTHER. Mind and Work. pp. 201. 1909. Doubleday, Page. $1.20.

A series of colloquial lectures on the habits of mind and body that should be observed in order to secure the greatest efficiency in our daily work. Important truths are vigorously put. We all should be better for following this advice.

KING, H. C. Rational Living. pp. 271. 1905. Macmillan. $1.25.

The applications of modern psychology to our daily living are discussed in President King's thoughtful style under four heads; the complexity of life, the unity of man, the central importance of will and action, the concreteness of the real. The treatment is much more philosophical than Gulick's, but equally practical for another type of mind.

MACCUNN, J. The Making of Character. pp. 226. 1900. Macmillan. $1.25.

A discussion in somewhat philosophical style of the elements that go to make up character, addressed to the parent and teacher rather than to the youth. The treatment is broad and thoughtful.

HISTORY OF EDUCATION

HINSDALE, B. A. Horace Mann. pp. 326. 1898. Scribner. $1.00.

Mann gave up law for education with the words, "Let the next generation be my client," and became the first great organizer of American education. A brief sketch of the previous development of education in America is followed by a well-balanced account of Mann's life and accomplishments.

**MONROE, PAUL. A Text Book in the History of Education. pp. 772. 1905. Macmillan. $1.90.

The most satisfactory history of education in English. The settings of the different periods and the contributions of the different tendencies are presented with clearness and force. At the end of each chapter is a brief bibliography of the general history of the period as well as of its educational work.

MONROE, PAUL. A Brief Course in the History of Education. pp. 409. 1907. Macmillan $1.25.

A condensation of the preceding for those who wish a briefer course. An effort has been made to retain the details where necessary to illustrate important facts. Teachers will find this a most excellent textbook, but should in all cases have the larger work for reference and for the bibliographies.

QUICK, R. H. Educational Reformers. pp. 568. 1890. Appleton. $1.50.

Sketches of leaders of educational thought from the time of the Renaissance to the present. Pestalozzi receives most space, 94 pages, and Herbart is omitted altogether. The sketches are written in vigorous style, with numerous quotations from the writings of the men in question.

TALBOT, E. A. Samuel Chapman Armstrong. pp. 301. 1904. Doubleday, Page. $1.50.

A life of the founder of Hampton College, which has done so much for the education of the Negro and the Indian. The breezy and rugged character of the man and the principles on which he based his work are illustrated by numerous quotations from his letters and sayings.

WASHINGTON, BOOKER T. Up From Slavery. pp. 330. 1900. Doubleday, Page $1.50.

The life story of a man who has overcome tremendous obstacles and accomplished wonderful things for the education of a race. He has been wise enough to give his people what they needed rather than what they thought they wanted.